THE TEACHER
IN EVERY PARENT

STRIVING FOR EXCELLENCE
IN ALL OF OUR CHILDREN

Joseph P. Smith

Credits

THE TEACHER
IN EVERY PARENT

STRIVING FOR EXCELLENCE
IN ALL OF OUR CHILDREN

Cover Design By: Anthony • Dee & Marie

Edited By: Lucy Hoffman

Design and Typesetting: By Ron Honoré

Published By: Four Aces Publishing Co.

ISBN-0-9674420-0-1

DEDICATION

I dedicate this book to my mother, Mrs. Ruth Ann Smith Harvey, whose love, devotion, and guidance have inspired me to be all that I am and everything I'm ever going to be in life. Abraham Lincoln once said, "All that I am I owe to my mother." Because of her my spirit and determination to succeed at anything I attempt will never die. This book is also for my son, Joseph, Jr. and my daughter, Jawanna. May you both realize your true potential in your lifetime. Thank you so much for growing up with me! Finally, this book is meant to pay tribute to their mother, Sonja. Without her love, understanding, and wisdom, the first chapter of our children's success would not have been possible. I love you all and may God continue to bless and enrich your lives.

Joseph Smith

ACKNOWLEDGMENTS

I would like to take this opportunity to thank my trusted lifelong friend, Lawrence Evans, whose counsel I have always sought and respected. To my high school counselor, Mr. Manuel Washington, who had the strength to confront, then turn me toward a new direction. To Mr. Burl Garnett, whose leadership and examples were the seeds that I used to grow as a man. To my father Willie L. Harvey who was there for me when times were rough. I am grateful to my valued mentor, Mr. Benjamin Wright, who showed me how to give something back to my community. To my brothers, Willie, Clarence, Kenneth, and Anthony; to my foster family, Marcus and Wilburt, for their love and support. Special thanks to Ms. Beverly Fletcher, for her thoughtful words of encouragement. Finally, a very special thanks to Dr.Anna Law whose continued encouragement proved invaluable to me. I'll never forget how she helped me. To Skies the Limit, Inc. and Ms. Lucy Hoffman for editing this book. My love and respect to everyone who helped me.

CONTENTS

INTRODUCTION

Delightful task, to rear the tender thought.
To pour the fresh instruction into a pure mind.
To breathe the enlivening spirit on
their heads and into their hearts.

—Thompson

Is there a more difficult and challenging job in the world than parenting? Can raising children who are functional parts of our society be amongst the most rewarding of all accomplishments as well? If there is a more monumental task in the world today, I've yet to meet it. I'm the proud parent of twin college-age young adults and in my nineteen plus years in this role, I have practically seen it all. The good, the bad and some of the ugly as well. It is my belief that parenting is the most important task of all! The primary reason for the writing of this short literary piece is to give something positive to other children and my community, in the hope enlightening some parents, while not boring any of them in the process.

I feel we must be parents to our children, first and foremost. If that responsibility isn't met directly or indirectly, we generally will regret it when they become young adults. I'm reminded of that old muffler commercial that I quickly incorporated into my own philosophy when it came to raising my kids.

It basically said, "You can pay me now or pay me later." Child rearing, for those who don't already know it is a long, slow process, many times yielding no day to day measurable results. To be done effectively and successfully, it has to be taken seriously. However, being committed in this manner doesn't mean parenting is not supposed to be a fun and enjoyable time in our lives as moms and pops. Moreover, it must be done by somebody.

In order to bring about positive results in any situation dealing with children, or even adults for that matter, we should be positive and repetitive. It is also important to find a way to measure our rate of success in this area. As most parents already know, this process will not always be an easy one to gauge. I have a relative who speaks with much pain and sadness regarding the terrible job he did as a parent. He speaks like many of us do, upon reflection—hindsight always being twenty/twenty. "If I had done this..... Perhaps if I had not done that"......Although there is no utopia where parenting is concerned, I don't know of any more rewarding accomplishment on earth than having smart, cool, well adjusted young people to unleash on our society in order to make this place a better one. Personally, if there is a more gratifying experience around, don't know what it is.

Let me say from the outset, I am not a scholarly figure with initials after his name. I don't have any heavy clinical training or credentials either. I'm just an above average person who, with the help of many people, effectively accomplished the difficult task of raising our children. After much trial and error I have also figured out a few things that I desperately wanted to share. During the writing of this book I never wanted to point the finger of blame in the direction of any parents. To begin with, being negative in this or any manner, does nobody any good. Parents parent, good or bad, the best way they know how.

I do feel however that many of my early parenting experiences can serve as short cuts for any busy parent attempting to raise well rounded, balanced children. Because of those experiences; I

Introduction

developed some thirty guidelines that I highlight throughout the book. During the discussing of my child rearing experiences I reflect with as much candor as possible regarding the events that shaped the lives of my wife and our children.

Because I was such a young parent to begin with (nineteen years old,) I will also share some of these strategies I utilized while raising my children, while being a kid myself.

Today more any other time that I can recall, parents are getting younger and younger. This translates into less prepared role models for our children to model. It certainly was a climate that wasn't always favorable for our children to be involved with. In the end however, (which is really the beginning) we did it! We crossed the finish line of preparing our kids for adulthood. They were ready to take on the responsibility of setting an example for other younger people to follow. That was our plan from the outset.

Very early in the parenting game, I realized that in dealing with children we must think on our feet while using common sense approaches. In conjunction with this, we need to also apply proven methods to solve small problems or challenges before they turn into major, negative events.

I believe that being unsure as parents about certain theories and having little or no practical child rearing experience sometimes causes us to question our own methods at the wrong time. Many times instead of second guessing ourselves, we should just go with our gut instincts and make decisions with conviction! In this manner, I believe that regardless of the outcome, the responsibility for success or failure is ours. We stay in control of the situation.

Times have certainly changed from even the time when I was a child. As a result, I hope to provide the benefit of my child rearing experiences in concert with those changing times: A basic, common sense approach together with a twenty-first century's child in mind.

The Teacher In Every Parent

Even though I don't attempt to pass judgment here, I also want to address all young adults who are contemplating becoming parents. Hopefully they will choose to rethink this important decision by weighing every available option before committing to this heavy responsibility. If they don't think about the totality of this decision, they are in my opinion being foolish people.

Many times, unfortunately this important decision is hurried into, sometimes with very little thought given to the matter. I believe young people should wait until they have developed and sustained close relationships with their spouses or mates first. Raising children should never be attempted the way we did it. In retrospect I deem our scenario to have been a stupid and selfish way to raise children. Decisions like these have put many of our kids at a distinct disadvantage today.

My other concern is the enormous amount of time needed for adults to acquire a solid financial foothold before starting a family. (Unless of course if they're born with a silver spoon in their mouths). Let's face the facts. It's difficult enough raising children when you are financially stable. In today's times, some smart planning and tougher financial times have dictated smaller families for many of us.

I also don't advocate starting a family until you have your own act together. However, for some of us that would mean we would remain childless. If the decision is to become parents anyway, we need to hone some fundamental parental principles. We will also need to align these principles with some basic, common sense to achieve maximum results. Once properly acquired, these skills should be used to encourage our children to become their absolute best.

In my quest to discover the elements involved in becoming a top-notch parent, I learned that there was a wide variety of parenting literature already written concerning the many

Introduction

components of parenting. Every parenting subject ranging from raising toddlers and teens, to single parenting, getting along with a new parent and even homosexual parenting had been published in an attempt to advise and counsel us on this most difficult topic.

There was so much material available that in my search for the most effective way to teach my own children, I began to develop brain-lock from information overload. All this new information was initiated by an explosion of new ideas and findings by child and behavioral psychologists of the late sixties and early seventies.

This new material has radically changed our knowledge base and philosophy regarding the relationship between our children and ourselves. Most of the changes that have occurred over the past three decades have not all been for the best. I also found in my research that many of these so called "experts" in the field of parenting generally expound directives based on their personal opinions. They depended solely on a particular theory, usually with only fragments of supporting data.

It is my belief that the best documentation of proof is how YOUR children are doing: If one were not a wealthy man they could hardly, with good conscience, discuss the components needed to become financially independent. Many clinical experts: (a) don't have children and as a result, rely on studies and theory, which I find a little odd. Some have children who: (b) have not developed as they had hoped using many of these new strategies. In my opinion, it's not by chance or happenstance that children turn out OK at maturity. Somebody has to be doing something right.

I further discovered that many earnest parents were clinging to these clinical books in search of the ideal child rearing experience for their own kids. Of course, we all want the best for our children. To that end, if there were an absolute proven method, every parent worth their salt would flock to it. There is no single strategy that can be implemented with total success. Unfortunately many professionals were selling their new methods falsely as absolutes. I believe this may have contributed to some of the rift that parents and children are experiencing today.

Another factor contributing to the division between parents and children today is the transient nature of our families. In the past we relied on the assistance of our parents and grandparents where child rearing was concerned. The original "village" that was at the core of bringing our children to maturity in America.

However as we became increasingly mobile, we began to relocate or transfer in the search for better career opportunities. We also sought other methods for raising our children. Day care centers and "how to" books quickly replaced the formidable extended family.

I once read a thought provoking quote by John Wilmot, seventeenth century Earl of Rochester. He said, "Before I married I had six theories about bring up a child and no children. Now I have six children and no theories." Most of the time where parenting is concerned, what we think we know, compared to what we actually know can be as wide as the Grand Canyon is deep. After all, we shouldn't be surprised when some of what we read doesn't work when we attempt it. In reality the most skillful of parents at times get taken for an emotional roller coaster ride by their children.

No book in the world can tell you everything about dealing with an obstinate child who is unyielding in their attempts to get their own way. Some new parenting methods may unknowingly encourage selfishness and self centered attitudes in our children as well. As a result, sometimes we end up with young people who are into instant gratification and who generally see the world from their point of view only.

Many times our children purposely do things to disrupt our

Introduction

families. Some children are painfully aware and are simply acting out for attention. Some haven't the faintest clue that they are causing any disorder in their family unit. Regardless, it's still our responsibility to do our best parenting, even if we face what seems like insurmountable odds.

As far as I'm concerned, part of our parenting problem is once we become adults we sometimes forget what it was like to have been a child. Just being aware of this is a powerful tool in bridging the parenting gap. We should realize that if a strategy doesn't work with our children right away it could mean 1) We are using the wrong method or 2) We haven't utilized the correct method long enough for it to be effective. This includes adjusting that correct method to fit your child specifically.

I wanted to target a certain age group with my material as well therefore, this work is designed to assist parents who have children ranging in age from five to fourteen. I use this cutoff age primarily because there is a brief time when our young people go into what I call 'shut off' mode. That is to say they don't want or think they need to hear anything you have to say!

I am of the opinion that if you have not reached them mentally and psychologically by then, there will be a different kind of learning involved for this type of kid. More on that later. This is, however, a large very important segment of our population and child base. As a tutor, mentor and parent, this age group is also the one with which I have the most experience and knowledge.

While writing this book, I was determined to keep my mind constantly focused on being practical, logical and realistic rather than theoretical or clinical. Not wanting to come off as an "expert" in this complex area was another goal of mine.

Today as in the past, theories can sometimes render themselves useless in dealing with the complexities of children of any age. It was important for me to use and discuss techniques, concepts and

The Teacher In Every Parent

practical ideas in order to solve many of the challenges that face our young people today.

My attempt was to write something that I thought people would find enjoyable and useful too, utilizing the guidelines that I developed and practiced. Again I have approximately thirty guidelines that are the highlighted points of reference. If you don't want to read the whole thing, just hit the guidelines! Notice how I use the term guidelines, not rules. Rules are made to be broken. Guidelines on the other hand, are made to be bent.

Let's admit it, things are more complex today than even a generation ago. For example, as a child I recall being able to receive only five available television channels. That being the case, I was content knowing that in our limited TV viewing time there would be specific weekly shows that would be seen. Knowing this just brought a certain amount of clarity to the day. For instance, Sunday was my Star Trek day. Wednesday was Gilligan's Island day. Friday was The Wild, Wild West day, etc. You get the idea. Our only alternative to watching television was going outside and playing some games.

Today, I often watch children 'channel surfing' over as many as sixty to seventy available channels. Most will agree that the expanded number of choices have created an inability for many children to make up their minds. The variety of options, once considered a favorable feature in any selection process, also serves to heighten the confusion in adults who haven't effectively learned proper decision making skills. Children are certainly no exception to this rule.

Since the media has such a dominating influence over us, I believe that it's necessary to turn the tables by getting control over it. Video taping selective shows for children is a great way to gain some control. Focus is extremely important in accomplishing any task, even if it is just completing something as trivial as watching a

Introduction

television show!

I have spent twenty years being a parent and a husband, enduring the many pains and pleasures of it all. I'm more convinced than ever that writing something such as this will prove beneficial to new and experienced parents alike. In the end however, it is about giving again in the hopes that other parents will gain new insight from our family's triumphs and tragedies.

Finally, I needed to share this practical, fun topic of parenting because it has gotten a bad rap. Hopefully this short book will make its way into the home library of every parent striving for the best in their children.

Thanks

ONE

REFLECTION

There are very few original thinkers in the world.
The greatest part of those who are called philosophers
have adopted the opinions of someone who went before them.

—Dugald Stewart

October 17, 1995

It was a balmy autumn afternoon as my plane began to descend into Washington, DC. In my only other trip to our nation's capital, I arrived by way of Dulles Airport, therefore as I approached National Airport, I felt somewhat lost as I came upon the busy terminal. After all, my last real visit to the District of Columbia was almost twenty years ago, on a combination recruiting trip and romantic quest. Neither situation worked out as planned and I never found much reason to go back east, even though my father lived on that side of the country.

Psychologically, I was very much removed from Washington, DC. anyway, a place we briefly stayed during my father's military tenure. However I was returning to visit my daughter, Jawanna Yvonne Smith who had decided to attend Howard University. She had departed three months earlier from Seattle, Washington.

I was pleasantly surprised that after spending her entire life in one location, she would be brave and daring enough to embark on a three thousand mile journey to continue her education.

She always said she would leave Seattle as soon as she possibly could. Although we didn't believe her at the time, her mother and I were pleased when she decided to do so.

Upon further reflection, I thought it ironic that I wouldn't have

1

The Teacher In Every Parent

gone this far to visit my long lost father since becoming an adult, but I would venture in a heartbeat to see my child. I was reminded that if a parent sacrifices time, energy and effort for a child, that child would generally reach their maximum potential. In short, they wouldn't let you down. Our children, Joseph and Jawanna had come through for us most of their lives. I suspect because we were always there for them. Something of course, that my father had never been for my four brothers or me.

As I approached the Howard University Campus in my rented car that I had received with only half a tank of gas, I was shocked by how much the area had changed. In this visit, like the last one, I decided to stay at the Howard University Inn. It was a hustling, bustling, thriving hotel back in the mid-seventies. As I spoke with the clerk, who was a Howard University junior, majoring in theater, she informed me that my stay would be the last weekend the Inn would be open for business. It seemed that poor management and the deterioration of the surrounding neighborhood had finally taken its toll on this landmark structure. Apparently, it was going to be renovated and turned into a college dormitory for incoming freshmen. As I later discovered, the dorms were already operating at only sixty-five percent of capacity so I didn't understand the logic for yet another one of these buildings. This appeared to be the last thing the university needed with enrollment down and the new university president already under intense scrutiny. Down the street I noticed the famed Howard Theater, once a Mecca for many black stars of the fifties and sixties, was now boarded up as well.

From what I remembered from two decades ago, the area had eroded greatly, both structurally and from a quality of life standpoint. Even as I absorbed all of the negative changes that clearly couldn't be ignored, I also knew that fine academic minds were continuing to venture to Washington, DC and thrive at

Reflection

Howard University. It appeared as though my daughter would be no exception. It was during my drive down Georgia Avenue headed toward the Smithsonian for lunch with an associate, that I reminded myself of the reason for deciding to write a book about the evolution of two young parents, two children and the internal and external family struggles they confronted, endured and overcame. I felt compelled to discuss the rough beginning and our maturing as young parents. I wanted to expand on the growth of our young children into functioning, independent adolescence. Finally, I had to discuss the collapse of a marriage but the survival of our family unit.

I also wanted to share some strategies that proved successful in raising our children during a very difficult time for them and ourselves. When our twins graduated from high school in 1995, it marked a significant personal achievement in our lives as parents. It marked the conclusion of one chapter as parents to our minor children and the awakening as parents of young adults about to make their own way in world.

Through our brand and style of parenting, our children were already making many of their own decisions and much of their own money. Jawanna was blessed with a twin brother, Joseph, older by five minutes. He was now a freshman at the University of Washington following an outstanding academic and athletic high school career. Joseph was our rebel in the Smith family, then and now. Being very intelligent and always striving to be different, his latest surprise was also the one that caused me the most distress.

It also marked a rather humbling athletic recruiting experience for him. Although his grades were solid, his size was not sufficient for him to continue playing his first love, which was football. The only scholarship offers he received to play football came from a small college in the state of Iowa. To our surprise his response to this offer was, "There's no way I'm going to Iowa to do anything.

The Teacher In Every Parent

I want to play in the PAC-10. I'll wait for one of those schools to call me." That call never came. He was rated by most big college sports publications on the west coast as a 'white chip,' not a blue chip or red chip, but a white chip. This generally meant that the athlete was either too slow or too small. Joseph had excellent speed, meaning his 'too' equated to 'TOO' small. At five foot seven and one hundred sixty-five pounds, he didn't impress any big time scouts. His dream of playing and starring for a top flight Division 1 program was now derailed. So attending the U. Dub (a familiar term for the University of Washington used by Washingtonians) was now a deviation from his academic and sport plans.

We were further bewildered by this decision because there were three baseball scholarship opportunities in California that were not used. Obviously we were not pleased with these recent decisions, although I could personally relate to a small portion of his reasoning...Dreaming....But why not CALIFORNIA dreaming?

Oh well, school was school, I guess. The young man was just hoping and wishing. Athletes do it unrealistically in their search for the illusive brass ring. We are taught that wishing is the first component of achieving. The fact that some athletes reach the pinnacle of these goals just magnifies the aspirations of being a top notch professional athlete even more.

As parents we didn't come from money, the old or new variety, so every little bit from any college or university would have helped immensely. That was why he was encouraged to attend school away from home...... Preferably at a school in California.

We had taught them from the age of six to think independently and critically. We also made it mandatory that they be held responsible for their decisions. Most of the time when you process the wrong information you make the wrong decisions. Obviously our son had made a colossal mistake! I believe a female was involved in this decision, although I'm not certain of it and Joseph never came totally clean with us.

Nevertheless, their mother and I were pleased that both of our young people were in college pursuing their education. Incidentally, Joseph is paying financially for this decision while attending school his freshman year.

Guideline Number One: You've got to pay the cost if you wanna be the boss.

Later that evening as Jawanna, Michelle her roommate and I sat in the dorm room of Baldwin Hall on the campus of Howard University discussing their new surroundings and some of the homesickness they both were feeling, I was struck with a sense of pride as I observed my daughter move about with a new found confidence. She was always an independent person, but this was a stark contrast from the meek, shy, introverted child who was afraid of making friends or being rejected in the first grade. My child had evolved into a young woman, complete with her own opinions and ideas about life.

Her roommate was Michelle Ross, a freshman from Lake Charles, Louisiana. She was a bright, articulate young lady who wanted to follow in the footsteps of her father who was a physician. They were describing a recent on campus attack of a student, so in spite of how impressed I was with my daughter's overall growth and development, I still insisted that they travel together whenever possible. Jawanna and Michelle seemed ideally suited as roommates. A far cry from my first roommate who was a redneck from Duvall, Washington, and who proudly informed me that he had never met a 'colored' person before.

Michelle had seen a picture of my son and through some conversations was beginning to develop an attraction for him. In explaining something about Joseph to her, I began to reflect on just how different our twins really were from each other. When they were younger Joseph was clearly the more outgoing and extroverted of the two.

Today he still is. A hyperactive and upbeat child, he was always more like his mother than he was like me. He made and dropped friends as quickly as she did. On the surface, Joseph and I shared a sports related bond with a gender based closeness that allowed him to comfortably challenge me without being offensive. We shared a very close relationship while growing up together. Even today, I love the manner in which he evaluates life and his role in it.

Jawanna adopted more of my personality traits however. It was always intriguing for me to observe these qualities developing in her. She was also always attempting to please me too, sometimes at her own expense. It was quite rare when we did disagree on a given topic. When we did have differences of opinion, it was usually pertaining the male company she was keeping. Although the kids were a matched set, our children were as different philosophically as night and day. However, they were still twins and occasionally those innate bonds would surface.

Joseph and Jawanna grew up very differently from the way Sonja and I did. We traveled extensively as children, which was completely different from our kids who were born and raised in Seattle, Washington. With the exception of summer vacations, they were complete Seattlelites. We were both the children of military fathers who had traveled and attended school in Europe, long before ever seeing the United States. Our families traveled extensively and regularly which meant we had no real roots.

My first memory of any real physical stability in my life occurred just before we were abruptly uprooted from it. We were dislodged from our traditional looking family in Raleigh, North

Reflection

Carolina on a cold November night.

"Mom, where are we going and where's dad?" I asked. "Shuh! Be quiet.... Get the suitcase from under the bed. Move! Quick!"
My mother had finally had enough of the beatings at the hands of my father. She was leaving him and taking all of us with her. When we arrived in his hometown from his last assignment in Frankfort, Germany, he assured her that our stay would be only for a few months. Once there however, he got comfortable with his North Carolina buddies and without consulting my mother, promptly changed his mind. He proceeded to isolated her by dictating her friendships and controlled her by not allowing her to work. Ruth Ann Elizabeth Smith was eight years his junior and yielded to many of his control tactics. The violence however was crossing the basic lines of decency. Charles, my father was Catholic and didn't believe in birth control either. We would have had many more siblings had it not been for my mothers sneak visits to a friends for daily contraceptives.

I didn't like it in Raleigh anyway. My second day of school a big guy approached me and said, "Hey nigga, what the hell you doing?" Coming from Europe, I was so naive I didn't know I was being called a derogatory name. I thought the guy just wasn't aware of my real name.

My response was, "Oh, my name isn't nigger. My name is Joe." With that he promptly punched me in the face. I ran home covered in blood! Two months later, I came home from school to find my mother crying. "What's wrong mom? Why you crying?" I inquired. "President Kennedy's been shot and killed," she said. "Oh, I'm sorry. Can I go out and play?" Just being a kid I guess. Anyway, something bad was always happening in North Carolina. This wasn't a great place for me and I knew it.

As my brothers and I rushed from the cab to a waiting Greyhound Bus, I was dazed, sleepy and confused. I was only

The Teacher In Every Parent

eight at the time. "Where were we going? Why wasn't dad coming?"

When we boarded the bus, I remember seeing a fancy logo of a long legged dog painted on the side of the building and a sign that clearly read, 'Relax and Leave the Driving to Us.'

Since then I have often wondered what would possess a woman to leave a man in the middle of the night with five boys, the youngest still in diapers. Her actions thirty years ago were those of a truly courageous and desperate woman.

As we grew older and began to ask specific questions about our father, my mother told us implicitly about being beaten by her husband, who was a borderline alcoholic as well as being a Christian. Through all of our discussions however, she never said a cross word about him to any one of us. Didn't allow us to either. It's clear to me that she still has much love for him, even today. I'm certain also from our conversations that my father was a man who fell victim to his circumstances. He was a good person, who was unfortunately weak and easily lead astray. Never forgetting the actions of my father, I realized that the only way I could get back at him for abandoning us was to promise myself I would always be the best parent I could possibly be.

Born on a military base in 1957 in Fairbanks, Alaska, I went to school in Germany and France before ever seeing the United States. We were stationed at Ladd Air Force Base. If growing up there was not tough enough, my older brother and I were transferring schools and cities every four or five months. I received an early start on learning about children, by simply being a curious and uncomfortable one.

I had my personality acutely developed and fostered through my insecurities of being a military brat, whose father was constantly being relocated from one military base to another and dragging his family with him. It appeared as though I was always

Reflection

the new child in class, and as a result, developed a thick, protective exterior that remains with me to this day.

I also learned a great deal about human nature and the human condition by observing all the many military children who attended school with me. After becoming an adult, I expanded my learning base by working as a volunteer coach, teacher and tutor dealing with all types of young people.

The first enterprise on that learning trail began for me as a young parent in 1980 when I was challenged by a mentor to give something back to the community that I had greatly benefited from. Benjamin Wright was that person, although I doubt if he really was aware that his presence had such an influence on me at the time. During that period, he was the only man I knew who could move freely from the corporate world to the inner city streets. African American people sometimes get labeled as corporate sell outs who are afraid to return to the neighborhood streets they grew up on after "making a success" of themselves. Sometimes the community is too harsh, setting unrealistic expectations of them. On the other hand, at times they are judged as incomplete individuals if they are unable to accomplish anything of note in the corporate world. As many of us know, some of the lack of successes stem from an uneasiness in dealing with European Americans and their unwillingness work with us in many cases. Ben had no such inadequacies in his personal agenda and I admired him for that. He was a street smart educator who related exceptionally well with young people. At the same time he advanced with much ease, interacting with business professionals and politicians alike.

After college, I attended a training program he co-directed and later assisted him, serving as an assistant peewee football coach. It was there I discovered that you don't really take from the communities you live in, you just borrow from them. You will pay those areas back in some way, shape or form at some point in the future. Another thing I learned from Ben, who I sometimes affectionately referred to as "the bear" because of his thick, muscular physique, was that a major part of giving back to your community included but was not limited to, raising children that you can be proud of.

As a former standout football player at the University of Puget Sound, Benjamin was a solid parent. I learned through watching him deal with his daughter Nadja, how to relate in the early stages with my own daughter.

Coming from a family with no sisters and a loving, but firm, drill sergeant for a mother, I knew how to deal with women, not daughters. My mother only occasionally allowed her feminine guard down. She was far too absorbed in managing the responsibilities of raising five boys to be feminine and thus appear weak. Through observing Ben's teachings and Jawanna's female charm, I learned a great deal.

In the early to mid-eighties he also coached some of the roughest, toughest, classiest and most successful young women's hoop teams that the city of Seattle has ever produced. His daughter Nadja was among that group.

His philosophy was a simple one, "When you step between the white lines you are no longer a girl, you're an athlete, and you will perform like one. After the game you become a young lady once again." A sound philosophy that I agree with and practice whenever I coach a group of females athletes.

I have always respected this mentor of young people and his parenting skills. I decided to raise my children in quite the same fashion. Once I arrived back to the Pacific Northwest, I decided to write this book. I sought and received the permission of everyone who had anything to do with raising Joseph and Jawanna. There were only going to be a few names used in the book because we

Reflection

handled a great deal of this on our own. I promised that nobody would be offended by this work in any way. This would be a labor of love, and the majority of comments would be complimentary. Most people were excited by the idea of being mentioned. The first portion of our parenting mission to raise children to functioning adolescence was complete. However, in developing young people, there still is much work to do.

TWO

POWER BALANCE

It must be borne in the mind that the tragedy of life does
not lie in not reaching your goals, the tragedy lies in
not having any goals to reach. It isn't a calamity to die
with dreams unfulfilled, but it is a calamity not to dream.
It is not a disaster to be unable to capture your ideas, but
it is a disaster to have no ideas to capture. It is not a disgrace
not to reach the stars, but it is a disgrace to have no stars to reach.

—Dr. Benjamin Isaiah Mays

July 28, 1978

I decided to become a full time parent to my twins and a husband to Sonja, although I hardly knew what that meant at the time. Putting the cart before the horse, like many guys I grew up with, I fathered my children before I was married. They were born during my sophomore year in college.

As my mother would later say to me, "Joe, you played with fire and got burned." She obviously was correct in this assessment although I didn't want to hear it. Most of the guys in my neighborhood were denying the existence of their children during this period, often implying that their girl friends were sleeping around and that the baby couldn't possibly belong to them.

This, in many ways, was a last ditch effort by the fellas in my group to relieve themselves of any moral or financial obligations. For whatever reason however, that thought never crossed my mind—any more than using some type of contraceptive did.

12

Power Balance

I always knew I was going to be a good parent. Although it took me a while to get over the fact that I was really only a nineteen year old kid who was about to become a father. At their birth, I found my children to be the prettiest, pinkest babies I had ever seen. Before that I though all infants were the ugliest of things; I knew nothing about newborns.

Someone had to inform me that a baby's true complexion was indicated by looking at their ears lobes. This came as a relief to me because at first, I thought somebody had pulled a switch on us at the hospital! That was not the only place my ignorance showed. I was unwise and confused about many personal things as well. I didn't even know what I was all about as a young man, and suddenly I had these two mouths to feed and clothe.

I wasn't very responsible in the beginning either, seeing my son and daughter once every couple of months or so. I had yet to accomplish my own individual goals, even though many of them were merely sports related. None of them were the caliber of this new and serious challenge that suddenly faced me.

I enjoyed debate classes in school and wanted to become an attorney. I was going to have a large, thriving practice. I was even going to do some pro bono work on the side knowing that charity is good for the soul. I also was a pretty fair athlete with designs on becoming a professional baseball player some day. I quickly found out while in college that I couldn't handle a hard slider or a cut fast ball. Anyway all of these plans had to be put on hold.

Guideline Number Two: When you bring a child into the world you must temporarily sacrifice your dreams for theirs.

Anyway, when I came home to visit my children, I found a very frosty reception at the King household. From the start,

The Teacher In Every Parent

Sonja's family circle was quite indifferent toward me and in the beginning, the feeling was quite mutual. They were a proud Pentecostal family, and the only other person who acknowledged my existence other than Sonja was her mother, Evelina. I would arrive in town and without making an appointment to visit the children, just show up. I knew the whole time that I would not be a welcome sight for anybody's sore eyes. Once inside I was quickly greeted with hostile stares and rude remarks. I endured the verbal attacks and even understood most of them. After all, Sonja was the oldest of the King children—The one that was supposed to set the pace for the other siblings to follow.

Born in Rocklind, Maine into a strict Church home she had in many ways, let the family down—Although nobody would come out and say it. Of course, "Truck," as she was affectionately known by her family, had many things going for her. She had been an excellent student and a superb track runner while attending Garfield High School with plans firmly set on attending the University of Washington and competing in Track and Field. A knee injury during her junior year destroyed any dreams she had for competing on the collegiate level. She attended the University of Washington, majoring in psychology, but was too busy being a single parent to her demanding twins to maintain any interest in much else.

While in town, I tried to do what I could to help. Since I was a struggling student with no money, I would take her to the laundromat to wash baby clothes.

What a humbling experience that was. You had to map out a strategy for getting the largest washers before anybody else could get them. That was the only way to save money. Racing around with quarters, we washed, dried and folded every stitch of baby clothing. In the beginning Sonja was so paranoid that if an item belonging to her twins ever hit the ground, it had to be re-washed!

Power Balance

I thought she was nuts. At times when she wasn't looking, I said, "God kiss it, Devil miss it," and quickly threw the item back in the basket. You know, like we used to do as kids when our candy accidentally dropped on the ground.

As the guilt of being an incompetent parent started to creep into my system, I began to search furiously for some answers to my dilemma. I loved Sonja, but thought I could be a good dad while remaining single. Some call it keeping your options open. What it was however, was pure and simple selfishness.

While returning from school I was struck by a thought so profound, that I was compelled immediately into action. I had become my father! A man who, whether intentionally or unintentionally, had abandoned his own family. This revelation was not an indictment of him, just an acknowledgment of the truth.

I instantly told my mother of my decision to marry Sonja and she responded by saying, "Now you're being a man, not just a pair of pants." You had to know my mother. She had a cliche for every event, and that day was no exception. I informed Ms. King and my bride-to-be in no romantic terms, of my intentions. It was also essential for me to let my future mother-in-law know that we would pay all expenses of our wedding. She would not have to endure any of the financial burdens accompanying this decision.

Traditionally the bride's parents pay for all of the wedding proceedings (with the exception of the honeymoon.) I figured since we had ignored many of the customs from the outset, that we should continue the pattern. Ms. King would have given us some financial assistance if we had asked for it. That's just the type of person 'King King' was.

Looking back, it was a little arrogant of me to assume that Sonja would even be interested in marrying me at all. I was fortunate however because she accepted my proposal. I left the details of the wedding to her, as is normally the case.

The small, quaint affair we had discussed became a huge spectacle of an event. I had to go out and find five groomsmen and a best man. I endured and even enjoyed most of the proceedings because it was clearly Sonja's day to shine. It was important for me that she bask in the pleasure of the day.

For my part, I was so nervous about losing my title of bachelor, I accidentally (or intentionally) went to my wedding without my tuxedo and shoes! My brother Clarence, who also served as my best man, was of little help to me on that terrifying day either. I believe he was more shaken by the event than I was, although he was already married. You would have thought he was getting hitched all over again.

It was a day of reckoning for me, time to become a man and a parent. There would be no honeymoon following the wedding. We didn't have the time or the money for any post wedding pleasures. Besides, we had already broken from tradition.

Guideline Number Three: Always do things
decently and in order.

Instead we went for a drive and parked at a site overlooking Alki Point, on the edge of Puget Sound in West Seattle and discussed our future. It was time to get serious about life and to start trying to take care of the tomorrows. That night we moved into our house, ate pizza by candle light, and started the difficult task of becoming a traditional, nuclear family.

We rented a nice three bedroom, two bath home in the Capitol Hill section of Seattle from a sweet old lady named Mrs. Johnson. Although she worked a regular job, she somehow managed to acquire five houses in the area. Mr. and Mrs. Johnson were quite a team. Mr. Johnson was a retired steelworker who comfortably

Power Balance

lived on his three pensions. She was a registered nurse at Group Health Hospital where she could be found assisting patients six days a week. Every other waking moment would find her at Long Acres, a racetrack formerly located in Renton, Washington. She always had plenty of money in her pockets.

She told me she had a system and used it to make a pile of dough, even though she would never let me in on her little secret. Just as well, I figured because I wasn't much of a gambler anyway. I had twin mouths to feed and couldn't run the risk of throwing money away on something that was not a sure thing. MJ, as she allowed only me to address her, was an amiable, gregarious, yet greedy woman who charged us more in rent than the house was really worth. Mrs. Johnson was a short, dark skinned, heavy set woman who was forever talking about something. She had happy eyes and a mouth full of tiny gold teeth. There was also a somewhat guarded side to her that prevented anyone from getting too close to her.

She kept insisting how much of a favor she was doing us, although the house had been vacant for nearly a year and there still was an outstanding mortgage on the property. I'm sure she was subsidizing it out of her own pocket until we came along. Upon reflection, I believe we were actually doing her a favor, rather than the other way round. During that time we provided her with some much welcomed and needed company. I related to her well because our personalities mirrored each others.

However, we parted ways when it came to her psychic side. She was a very superstitious woman who believed in palm reading, tarot cards, psychic readings and curses. This stuff scared the hell out of me. Most people thought she also believed in witchcraft as well, but I never would believe that. I just thought she was an eccentric old person who was selfish and opportunistic in her approach to life.

The Teacher In Every Parent

Secretly I believe she was just a lonely old lady who needed some company.

At the time of course, I was more interested in how we were being perceived by the Johnson's to do any critical evaluating. We probably looked like a pitiful sight to them. Two young parents with a ready made family and not much else.

Over all, however, I enjoyed her company and frequented their home often. At times I found myself acting as mediator for their lively family debates. She didn't get along with her husband, but we thought he was a delightful man. Mr. Johnson also played a great Santa Claus for the children. I was too skinny to be an authentic St. Nick. In the process of befriending her, I persuaded her to allow us to use a percentage of the five hundred dollars per month rent we were paying toward a lease option purchase. After much pondering she agreed. (My mama didn't raise any fools.)

As I set forth on the road of being a husband and father, I quickly discovered that my children desperately needed us to be powerful parents. However, before we became these powerful, prepared parents, I needed to know what power, as it related to the structure of a typical family was all about.

Oxford's Dictionary lists thirteen separate elements of power. It uses synonyms to describe power in both positive and negative ways. For example, it speaks of productive power: The effort used in achieving excellent results and reaching goals. It also address the stagnant power of weakness, inaction and complacency: Negative power. For the type of young people that we were striving to develop, obviously positive power needed to be instilled IN US FIRST and utilized by us on a daily basis, before applying it to our children.

Early on I realized that a child first admires, then mirrors everything they view consistently. I was aware of this because I

Power Balance

had witnessed, then copied many of the traits of my mother and grandparents as they unconsciously used many teaching techniques with us. From the start my children didn't adjust to my style of parenting and followed their mother all over our house. They even pursued her into the bathroom. That was either love and devotion, or I was a pretty bad parent. Looking back, I'm not sure which it was.

The initial reason for their uneasiness was that they were watching other children in the day care they were attending receiving practically everything they desired. Our children couldn't understand why they were being raised in a different manner. I was attempting to teach them discipline and patience by allowing them to earn what they received.

This method was similar to the one I had experienced as a child.

Although I knew I was on the right parenting track, I was not enduring myself to my kids. Even though I was encouraging my children, all the checking and correcting was not making me a very popular guy around my house. Fortunately for me, Sonja sensed my growing frustration with the situation, while admiring my effort. The blessing was that she shared the same goal of wanting to produce independent, self sufficient young adults who were capable of surviving and thriving in this ever changing world of ours.

Without really knowing it, she set us all down and conducted our first family meeting. In this unofficial get together we reinforced the love and respect that we shared for our children.

We also stressed the importance of their understanding my reactions to their behavior when they were not doing the things expected of them. When our children heard that I really loved and cared for them, they responded immediately and positively. We had established a delicate power balance in our family. I learned

The Teacher In Every Parent

the power balance between the parents and the children in the early years does not have to be fifty-fifty. In the beginning, you want to establish a balance that is comfortable for your family. Sometimes it can be eighty-twenty; at times it can be sixty-forty; still other times, the balance may be set at seventy-thirty.

The important aspect is that the parents or guardian control the family structure. It may sound harsh, but someone has to be in charge! In any marriage, the same power balance exists, to a lesser degree. I'm not aware of any relationship or marriage where a fifty-fifty climate exists. Generally, one partner garners more control during any given situation than the other partner does. In a normal setting this power balance generally switches back and forth. Depending on the skill level and situation involved, a man can easily take a back seat to the woman. (And in many cases should.)

As a result of our learning, then sharing this information with our children, I was now a firm believer in these family meetings. More on that later.

Although neither Sonja or I were not raised in this manner it was important for us to determine in advance the type of children we wanted to produce prior to developing it. In this way, we were encouraged to make some tough early decisions in their lives and get their cooperation-something that would prove beneficial as the years went by.

Even though we knew we needed to become powerful parents in order to be successful ones, the impetus to do so was thrust upon us quite by accident. We enrolled our children in the first grade at the age of four because they were bright and like many of the parents of our day, we were going to get an early jump on their educational process.

Our vision was that they were going to be brilliant students, graduate high school at fourteen, then enter college.

Power Balance

They were intellectually advanced for their age. I had read somewhere that reading to expectant mothers increased the intelligence of the fetus being developed. It made sense to me because a child will generally carry any negative scars with them into the world, so why not the positive ones? I tried it. It really worked! They were also raised in a progressive daycare called Kings Learning Center, conducted by their grandma King. Several mind-stimulating activities were stressed on a daily basis. I believe this combination enabled them to fall in love with reading and learning as I had.

They had been taught to read with the use of phonics as the learning tool. We taught them math and science (solar system) through interactive learning games on our personal computer. It was somewhat primitive by today's standards, however, very effective. They were taught interactive and social skills by playing board games. As a result, we didn't perceive a jump-start in their formal education would be a problem for them, although later it would become one.

Guideline Number Four: Experiment with new ideas for your child. You may strike gold.

A child should have a positive and wonderful introduction to any school system. Hopefully, their teacher will be able to locate any areas of concern and address them early on. When I mention this, certain concerns come to mind such as hearing and speech difficulties, perceptual problems or perhaps any behavior concerns. We were not as fortunate when it came to this stage.

Their school was a kindergarten through fourth grade setting, located in the working middle class Mount Baker neighborhood of South Seattle. They were enrolled in the first grade and we thought our children would be taken care of because of the

The Teacher In Every Parent

perceived wholesome school environment.

We knew that both of our children were reading above first grade level before they started school, even though Joseph spoke with a lisp and wasn't easily understood. Unfortunately for them, after we enrolled them, we became pre-occupied with work and didn't ask how our children were doing.

Thinking back on that time, I don't know how we could have been so stupid. If I could use the analogy of planting a garden to preparing a child's mind for school, I'll show you just how dumb we were. Our children were the seeds and were planted and nurtured while still in the womb. They were then fed the fertilizer of knowledge through being taught reading, science, and mathematics skills. Later, we bathed them in the sunshine of courteousness, self-respect, and respect for others. Then we lifted the protective veil and exposed them to the locust! We did what most well-intentioned parents do. We expected the school system to continue to teach our children the way we had. In effect, we just stuck our heads in the sand for a while.

When we resurfaced, it was April. Ms. Jones, our children's teacher, had requested a conference with us. At the meeting the teacher would say, "Mr. and Mrs. Smith, according to the reading test, Jawanna is reading on a third grade level, well over our requirement. However, Joseph does not seem to be able to read yet."

We just looked at each other initially, not really knowing what to say. We knew he could read as well as his sister and were puzzled by her statement.

I finally asked, "Well, Ms. Jones, we know he can read so what you're saying is news to us. She said, "Why then is he not reading in my class if he can read?" "I don't know. Did you ask him?" To that she replied, "No, I just assumed he couldn't so I had to give him a failing grade in reading. Well, it's not actually a failing

Power Balance

grade, just an N for Needs Improvement." "No problem," Sonja chimed in. "We'll get that grade changed tomorrow, as soon as we have him read for you. He can read better than his sister."

To that Ms. Jones said, "Oh, if that can be done, I'll be more than happy to change the progress report from Needs Improvement to Satisfactory." To which Sonja responded, "No, after you hear Joseph read, you'll change it to Outstanding!"

"Maybe so. By the way, Mr. and Mrs. Smith, your children seem to be having some problems on the playground because of their size. They're a little small for six and some of the other children occasionally pick on them."

Sonja, who was always oversensitive about the children's size, stood up and sternly said, "They're not six, they're four and a half.

If you had taken the time to look at their records, you'd know that!"

"Oh, they're advanced students. I see. Well, that explains their size," the teacher said. Sonja was seething by this time. She got up and stormed out of the room.

"Don't worry," I said. "Everything will be straightened out tomorrow. I just have one question for you. Why didn't you inform us about this earlier? We've been coming to all of the PTA meetings and open houses."
She looked at me in a rather curt manner and said, "You never asked me about it, Mr. Smith."

As it turned out, Joseph could read well, but was not easily understood because of his lisp. He felt embarrassed because of it. He didn't want to read aloud, causing the teacher to assume he was not able to read. We learned a valuable lesson about parenting from that experience. We thought the teacher was going to look out for our children so we slacked off our parental responsibility.

The teacher, while not incompetent or uncaring, chose not to go the extra mile before drawing her conclusion. This left me with the understanding that children are not the only ones who seek the path of least resistance. It was easier for her to say and do nothing rather than to discover a potential problem that she might have to help solve. The lesson was learned, categorized and used positively.

Guideline Number Five: Actively involve yourself in your child's education.

From then on, we never took that aspect of our power parenting responsibility for granted. Until we finally removed our children from the public school system, we interviewed teachers and schools on a regular basis. Furthermore, we developed a simple rating system, and when a teacher or school didn't measure up, our children would never enter that classroom or school building.

Another criterion we incorporated was the classroom seating theory. I had recently read some material that discussed academic achievement and its relationship to classroom seating locations. In this study conducted by the Developmental Learning Center, a direct correlation between front position seating, classroom learning and good grades was shown.

In most kindergarten—fourth grade school settings at John Muir Elementary, teachers had seating assignments that were structured according to alphabetical order, meaning that the S for Smith put our children near the back of the class. We always insisted that Joseph and Jawanna sit in the first quarter to third of every classroom, without exception. When pressed, most teachers would make this simple concession. Occasionally, we would come across an acceptable teacher who was firm on her seating arrangements. I would always suggest a coin flip. Having developed a rapport with the teacher, this was easily done.

Power Balance

I still have that two headed coin in my safe deposit box.

Very few teachers and administrators believed we were a little overbearing. Most of them, however, liked and appreciated our efforts because most parents had abandoned this important aspect of parenting.

In the early years (3-10), a great deal of parental power needs to be positively applied in the direction of our children for <u>their</u> benefit. Many parents are attempting to raise their children with good intentions, but very little direction. I believe that to locate this direction and for parenting to be effective, there needs to be some element of control in the power balance. This is the only way responsible parenting can exist. It's okay to want the absolute best for your child, however it is a gross miscalculation to assume that, without setting and enforcing boundaries, your child will know which path to travel.

The goal of every parent should be for their child's true potential to be realized. For that to occur, a parent must set the ultimate example, then direct the child. Remember, children mirror what they witness on a regular basis. Our children will be the winners when we utilize our good judgement and correct parenting methods.

Guideline Number Six: Don't expect others to do what <u>you</u> are supposed to do.

To become these effective power balance parents, we also needed to take a personal inventory of our own strengths and weaknesses. Then we could combine forces in order to compliment each other. In our situation, for example, in the early stages of our marriage, Sonja was far more effective in dealing with people than I was. I observed the innate intentions or body language of those same people a little better than she did. I always

The Teacher In Every Parent

suggested she blended better with people because she was less aware of their true intentions than I was.

Think about it. If you could be a fly on the wall and know what an individual really thought about you, would it change how you dealt with them? Probably so. It did with me. Reading people is something of a gift with me.

At any rate, whenever we did business in person, for the most part, she did the most of talking and I put my internal barometer to good use. That worked extremely well, even with my big mouth. The only exception was during school conferences.

The idea of blending strengths worked well for us regardless of the occasion. Whether it was planning an event, managing the house money or communicating effectively with our children. Furthermore, whichever parent was better in a particular category, THAT parent was charged with leading in that area. Plus, they must teach the other parent or guardian in order to increase their skills. The supporting parent was charged with the responsibility of learning as much as possible by being a strong, sustaining supporting person at all times.

This joining of strengths also works well in non-traditional parent situations. It had better because today 6 out of 10 households are headed by single parents and the responsibility of instruction in many cases is shared by others. Grandparents, aunts, uncles, and friends often assist parents in child rearing.

As the experimenter, innovator, and the dreamer in our household, I read practically every book and attended almost every business and self-improvement seminar that came to town. During that time, I often brought home some bizarre ideas. No matter how crazy some of them were, Sonja was always the calming, practical, influential supporter that I required to pull some of those things off.

We never smoked, rarely drank or used foul language in the

presence of our children. I would occasionally give dinner wine to the kids however. My wife thought I was creating alcoholics. Of course there was always a method to my madness. My grandmother used to say if you give them "a little taste" when they are child, they generally won't crave it as adults. I found it to be true although I don't recommend giving alcohol to children.

When we disagreed with each other, they usually witnessed us debating instead of arguing, compromising instead of dictating. When all else failed, we simply flipped a coin.

We taught the kids about drugs by bringing the stuff home and laying them out on the coffee table. Everything from marijuana and hashish to hallucinogenic drugs were put on our table for their street education. This education also included alcohol, which was the most dangerous drug of all.

During this drug education, I was receiving these drugs from acquaintances who were from the streets dealing. I had attended high school with many of them and most hadn't progressed a day past graduation.

At the time, Sonja believed I was doing the wrong thing and thought our children would grow up to be drug addicts. She was taught through the church that insulating a child from drugs was the best protection. Although I believe in most of the teachings of the church, I knew that knowledge and discipline were the only way to prepare a child of God to overcome these temptations.

Part of this education included discussing with them why some children start experimenting with drugs in the first place. We talked about many of them having weak or absent fathers. We also told the kids about overprotective and overindulgent parents, as well as the affect hostile or fighting parents had on them. Finally, we discussed parents with unrealistic aspirations for their children. As our kids began to realize, parents were the primary element in determining whether children would turn to drugs.

The Teacher In Every Parent

As we taught the "do's" and "don'ts" of the streets, I later counseled them about the actions they should take if they met with any of their friends experimenting with drugs. They were instructed not to intercede if they witnessed their friends doing drugs: Just leave the scene, fast! As parents, when we discovered a playmate who was not on the same page (from a lifestyle standpoint) as our children, we would subtly intercept and replace that child with another. This may sound a bit cold, however, I was never bothered by my decision-especially in the beginning stages of our children's lives.

As a result, our children have never desired to do anything drug related. They don't even like aspirin. They also would instinctively drop a friend or acquaintance once they discovered they were using drugs. Today, however, they would encourage a friend to seek help, while supporting them the best way they could.

We had clear objectives for Joseph and Jawanna. We introduced them to sports because it was something they expressed enjoyment in. We also did it because we knew drugs and athletics normally mixed like oil and water!

Intervening does not mean dominating or controlling our children or the household in a dictatorial fashion. We used power parenting as a nurturing process of checks and balances that kept our children constantly abreast of how they were doing as we encouraged them to reach for excellence.

Guideline Number Seven: We need to learn to control the situations that involved our children.

As stated earlier, there is a power format operating in every home and our children are normally observing it and making mental notes. They will first notice which parent seems to be in

Power Balance

charge of addressing most situations and how both parents interact with each other in a shared power format. During their observation period, they will be checking out how well their parents work together to solve problems. This is a crucial time because eventually they will model our actions.

With further examination, they will determine which parent to approach when they want something, whether it's special attention or an extra treat. They always seek the easiest or most accommodating parent to deal with because their goal, like that of most children, is to get exactly what they want! That's okay and quite normal.

The problem arises when a child doesn't receive what they want, as well as no explanation for not receiving it. Many of these children grow up taking from others and robbing because they feel a need to have these material items immediately. If you were to investigate their past, you would probably find that these children were either granted everything they wanted by overindulgent parents or received very little to nothing, with no explanation, by strict, overbearing ones.

In watching, our children also learn to manipulate and divide us. Don't ask me where they picked that up from. (Us of course!) Even though it was tough to manipulate me, I did fall victim to the old "divide and conquer" method at times. The classic scenario went like this:

Either child: "Dad, can I go outside and play?"
My response: "Not right now. I think you have some homework to do."
Either child: Ignores response, finds mother and asks same question. This time gets the desired response.
Twenty minutes later, I notice the child outside having a good ole' time!

The Teacher In Every Parent

Dad: "What are you doing out here?" Completely blown away by the shear defiance of my child's actions.
Child: "Oh, it's okay, dad. MOM said it was all right."

Division and debate sometimes commence. If a child can get their parents to question each other's action, they win! So, being a united front in any situation is always the best approach.

Guideline Number Eight: Parents, get on, and remain on the same page at all times.

In the beginning, our children tried this stuff all the time. I thought it was perfectly normal for them to attempt it and perfectly normal for us, as parents to be ahead of their game. Later, however, our children rarely questioned our decisions or attempted to pull the wool over our eyes. Even if they did not like the policy, as long as we were together in our decisions and didn't show any signs of weakness, we were just fine. Besides, I used to have an innate ability to feel when my children were up to something. It was just a little rumbling in my stomach, and I would always act on it. I believe this came from the closeness developed over much time spent together. They thought I had a sixth sense! I did. I believe they call it "mother wit."

Finally, I discovered we all should parent as though the CEO of the firm was watching us. Individuals should teach their children as though the company's bottom line was at stake and they have to answer to the stockholders.

Many of us have experienced an employee who works at one pace when the boss is away and at another pace when he/she is looking over their shoulder. None of us should parent in this manner. People, especially children, are far more important than any career interest. However, many times we pay more attention

Power Balance

to our jobs than to our children. While careers are an important part of being an adult, we need to remember that parenting is our number one job. In the balance of power, we must lead our children and set the ultimate example while expecting them to follow. We then become the ultimate power parent.

THREE

QUALITY TIME

Dost thou love life? Then waste not time,
for time is the stuff that life is made of.

-Benjamin Franklin

Spring 1980

Once at a seminar I heard a speaker ask, "What's the one thing that a rich man and poor man have in common?" His answer: "They both have only 24 hours in a day." True enough. We both have the same amount of time. Imagine that—Warren Buffet and me! Bill Gates and me! H. Ross Perot and me! Well now. No matter how much financial wealth a person has, his time is a limited commodity.

How we choose to use our time is up to us. It's our decision. Quality time is described as the qualified act of investing our available time wisely in some pursuit, in the hopes of yielding a handsome return in the future. Whether it's quality time spent on our golf game, our book club or the raising of our children, one thing is clear: Time in any activity with a good dose of passion will normally yield some measure of success! As it relates to our families, time is the single most important ingredient in building and maintaining healthy relationships. Everything required for effective communication with our children or spouses involves time.

In order to effectively discipline and guide our children, we need to spend enough time to develop a rapport with them

Quality Time

initially. In this day and age, we are so busy that we are not able to give our children the amount of time needed for them to prosper. Maybe it's a lack of dedication and commitment. Sometimes, for whatever reason, we only give a limited amount of our time to this important pursuit. I believe that to justify not giving enough time to our children, we sometimes refer to the limited time spent as "quality time." That's just my point of view however, I believe I'm correct in my opinion.

Anyway in our society there are many things in which we find value. Of all the valuable items in the world, time, which is this intangible commodity, is the most precious of all. It's often said that time is the only true measure of equality in our world today. How we utilize it is up to us. I believe it is sometimes misdirected.

Let me give you an example. Fifteen years ago, personal computers, facsimile machines, pagers, cellular phones, and other electronic devices were supposed to save us so much time that we would have more of it to spend with our loved ones. We were even supposed to see a reduction in the average work week because these electronic gizmos would increase our productivity and thus give us some of our precious time back. Computers were even supposed to allow us to work from home, giving us more time with our families.

While in a few companies working from home is possible today, the fact is that with corporate mergers, acquisitions and job duplications, those of us fortunate enough to be employed are generally spending more and more time with these <u>toys</u> and less time with our families. We are now actually working more and receiving less. Less money, less rewards, and less satisfaction.

One parent expressed the problem to me like this: "There is never enough time to get everything done at home that needs to be done. It's the same on the weekends. Just about the time I feel I have everything done in my home and want to settle down with the children or do something for myself, it's Monday morning again!" In fact, my studies showed me that of the three major challenges parents cited, a shortage of time topped the list when it came to parenting.

In order they were:

Lack of time.
Feeling too much parental guilt.
Illness and fatigue.

These complaints came from the two-parent households! TIME................the major dilemma.......where is it best spent......at home, work, with our families or on ourselves. You can generally do only two things with it. You can waste it or invest it. Use it or abuse it. While working in the investment business, I handled the accounts of several clients who were very wealthy.

One man, in particular comes to mind. In the three years we handled his business, this man had never come in to visit me. Outside of his financial portfolio, the only thing I knew about this gentleman was that he was elderly, widowed and wealthy. Once, to my surprise, he came in to discuss some of his investments with me. He was a feeble-looking man, carrying a cane in one hand and dragging an oxygen tank in the other.

During our meeting, I kept thinking, this guy has all the money anyone could ever want, but it won't do him much good because at 87 years of age, he's practically out of time. We can typically spend a lifetime earning and accumulating money or items money can buy, and not be able to fully enjoy them.

Although the importance of time is undeniable, it is usually limited in most of our families. After we meet our commitments of jobs or careers, church, and community responsibilities,

Quality Time

sometimes there is precious little of it left for the family.

In dealing with our family relationships in general and parenting in particular, time is equally important. However, we are limited to but a few short years of solid involvement in the lives of our children as they are growing up. Before we know it, they are gone from the nest and well into establishing lives of their own.

In the average family, our children are only with us one-half of their first eighteen years of life and approximately one-third of that time is spent sleeping! Given our limited time frame, the question is how much time should a parent spend with their children? How much time is the right amount? This is an impossible question to fully answer. However, one thing is certain, many children are being short changed today. They just are not receiving their fair share of the available time.

The amount of time a child needs to develop to their optimum capacity can't be measured in hours per day. It can only be measured in a child's psychological, physical and emotional well being. It varies from one child to another and the quantity of commitment needed is enormous as problems can occur when certain time commitments are not met.

Sonja told me once that many adults think they're doing a good job of parenting, but are disappointed when their child doesn't meet their expectations. She concluded that the missing ingredient was the lack of time spent with the child in the early years. She believed some parents miscalculated the actual amount of time they spent with their kids. She believes a parent must sacrifice everything and give to their children totally. I didn't share her philosophy completely. However, regardless of the level of time involved, we both concur that the more time given to a child early on, the higher the realistic expectations can and should be.

The Teacher In Every Parent

According to Kay Kuzman, author of <u>Prime Time Parenting</u>, the ideal time to conceive children is between the ages of twenty-three and thirty. Unfortunately, this is also the time when most of us are finishing school, establishing careers, and generally buying (charging) everything it took our parents a lifetime to accumulate. Ironically, parents are the busiest during the very years their children's needs are greatest!

Add to that a source of much concern to me: The fact that as individuals we are generally not the sharing, sacrificing people our parents were. This has created a problem concerning the difference between quality and quantity time. If one agrees with the idea that children, especially those in the early years of life, require a great deal of time, why then should we call it quality time and not quantity time? Does this imply that the other time spent is not quality time? In my opinion, all time is valuable regardless of the task, and therefore, all time is quality time. I believe the use of the term "quality time" implies that a majority of parent's time is being spent elsewhere. I discovered that many parents who had their time focused in these other directions simply referred to the remaining time as "quality time." This is probably a mistake, since to accomplish most things with a child, a great deal of time is required. Since all time is priority time, and we all have busy schedules, there needs to be solid agendas set and followed when doing everyday activities with our children. Be on the lookout for conflicts that can occur when ambitious working parents leave their children for long periods of time and constantly choose job responsibilities over family obligations. If this is done long enough, eventually the children may grow to resent their parents and whatever it is they spend the majority of their time doing— Even if it is working and attempting to provide the best for them.

These children will also question the parent's love for them. Once during the summer, I worked in a nursing home and witnessed this first hand. My job was to direct and engage the elderly residents during the daily activity hour. This time generally consisted of stretching, walking, and other forms of physical movement.

I had an opportunity to get to know many of these wonderful people and found them to be a delightful group. I could not understand why they didn't have many visitors. In fact, some of the adult children of these elderly folks who did occasionally drop in, were downright evil to towards their parents. Being the curious type and while receiving some "none of your business" type responses, I discovered from the adult children that many of these delightful old people had been terrible and neglectful parents. Many of their children had no remorse in treating their parents in the same manner. While revenge shouldn't be the necessary response here, it sometimes is. You normally reap what you sow.

Guideline Number Nine: Give the amount of time to your child today, that you expect to receive from them tomorrow.

My own children were jealous and resentful of me for a short period regarding the amount of time I spent with them. As a result of my mother's love of children, after we were grown, she began taking in kids who were wards of the court on a temporary basis. In 1984 she had two foster children living with her and whenever possible, I would take them off her hands. We would all do things together as a family. After a while, my children, (especially Joseph) confronted me about amount of time we were all spending together.

"Why are these guys always hanging around us? They're not in our family! Why are you always taking them with you and buying them something special?" he inquired.

Needless to say I was surprised, both by their concern and his tone of voice. I had to remind myself that he was only eight years old and felt threatened by these two boys.

Later I explained to them that these two little guys, who were eight and ten respectfully, had lived a brutal life. After telling my children that these two had witnessed the murder of their father, and that their mother was a drug abuser who had abandoned them, they were stunned. I went on to inform them that they were made wards of the state and had been in several foster homes throughout the years. I concluded with, "The very least we can do is make any time they spend with us an enjoyable experience." They slowly began to understand, and today Marcus and Wilburt are loved by all of us. They are like my sons and like brothers to Joseph and Jawanna. They were fortunate enough to stay with my mother, Sonja and me until they reached adulthood. All of us learned that you must give and share something in order to receive it in return, even if it's your valuable time.

To take full advantage of any available time, consider occasionally taking your children to work with you so they can expand their knowledge base of what you do when you're away from them. Many times they will gain a greater appreciation for your hard work and may be more willing to assist you at home. You'd be surprised at how many kids have no idea what their parents or guardians do for a living! I don't mean just taking them to work when the annual day suggests it: "The Take Your Daughter to Work day." I hired my daughter to type and stuff letters for me on Saturdays for five dollars an hour when she was eleven. This created a fantastic opportunity for us to share some valuable time with each other. She also learned a greater appreciation for working and being productive. She saw first hand what I did when I left home. Occasionally Joseph would

Quality Time

help but by this time he was already employed in the real world. Financial wizard and a long distant mentor of mine, Charles Givens taught me the secret of hiring a family member. We used this method as a legal tax write off as well. Givens is such a smart man.

There is another disturbing piece of news that haunts some parents. Everyday thousands of children arrive home from school to an empty house. Weekly, hundreds and hundreds of parents make the decisions to leave their children home alone while they go to work, run errands or even attend social functions. It's estimated that about 40 percent of all children are left home at some point in time. In many extreme cases, children are left alone so often without a parent that these children are labeled, "latch key children." In my day, the house key was visibly strung around the neck. I know this because I was one of them. When I arrived home, my responsibility was to my younger brothers until my mother arrived. That's just the way it was. There was not much of a networking system around then and not many available activities. I just baby-sat and received an occasional reward for a job that was completed successfully.

The popular movie "Home Alone" and it's sequel, has portrayed a child's survival skills in a very humorous but unrealistic manner. Macaulay Culkin is seen cleverly outwitting and outsmarting two would-be burglars. During all this mayhem, we have these confused, unsuspecting parents who are not even aware that their son is missing. The film is cool, cute, even funny but quite unrealistic. The realities facing children who find themselves home alone are very different from that.

There are many issues, potential risks and dangers that we should consider before we place a child in that situation. Fortunately, Joseph and Jawanna had an extended family and rarely had to stay home alone until they were about twelve.

The Teacher In Every Parent

I was approximately eleven years old when my mother would leave me with the care of my younger brothers. The legal age for most of the country was twelve. We were illegal; Sorry mom. Anyway she helped me compile this list. The issues that concerned her the most were:

*Age readiness
*Clear parental rules and expectations
*When and how to answer the telephone or doorbell
*How to contact parents or other adults in case of emergency
*Responsibilities for siblings
*Use of unstructured time (e.g. watch TV, video etc.)
*Where the emergency phone numbers are located
*Friends coming to the house
*Access to "adult" cable TV

There is also a level of expectation that a parent should have for a young adult. Older adolescents are usually responsible enough to manage alone for limited period of time. With the busy schedules that sometimes confront parents, it's not out of line to solicit the help of an older son or daughter. Of course a parent should consider the child's maturity and past behavior in certain situations of responsibility when leaving them alone. In our family, Joseph and Jawanna were expected to watch out for one another at all times. We always believed that "blood was thicker than water," and that the responsibility for family members came before anything else. One of the few times I remember spanking Jawanna was when at the age of five, she found a new friend. (A twenty—minute-old friend!) Together they began beating up Joseph. We didn't have any tolerance for that type of behavior even at five.

We also encouraged age appropriate behavior from the kids through placing them in situations that would make them step up

Quality Time

and act accordingly. In evaluating them, we established that their emotional growth was on par with their chronological age. Therefore they were placed only in those situations that we felt they could handle.

My mother used to say, "Don't let me find out you know how to do something, because you will then own that responsibility." I didn't totally agree with her philosophy. However, I didn't see anything wrong with requesting and expecting a family member to come through for their family. Especially if as parents, we are doing everything possible for them.

Some children's emotional growth and level of responsibility are ahead of their chronological age. Sometimes they are behind. Either way a parent should know precisely what level the child is at and slowly introduce them to new, more challenging environments. At times, we would just leave and test our children. In the house I grew up in, the phrase was, 'I'm going to try you.' As a result, I'm was a firm believer in finding out what kind of child I really had. Perhaps it would be a quick trip to the store or just going around the block a couple of times and checking back—No longer than fifteen minutes; Time enough to evaluate their actions. Then we could determine what situations to entrust them with.

While I realize that the optimum utilization of time is a very difficult proposition, some basic concepts can be used to make this process simple. As easy as this sounds, many of these things just aren't done!

1) Develop a routine - First of all, when children know what to expect, they are better equipped to assist us. It saves precious time when there are preset assignments and responsibilities.

The Teacher In Every Parent

2) Establish your priorities -(Something we did not do very well.) We paid special attention to our children and their needs. This was after all our responsibility. However, we neglected what we had begun in the prior years; We stopped providing time for each other. It's my recommendation that once a month you find a suitable baby sitter and allow a weekend just for your mate. In addition, find some time to get in touch with yourself to recharge your own battery!

3) Limit non family social activities - When our children were younger, if they weren't welcome at a social function, we did not go either. Don't be afraid to ask, "Mind if we bring our child along?" Sometimes kids aren't allowed. It doesn't hurt ask. We also belonged to clubs or organizations that were youth oriented. We planned social activities that included the family. That does not mean that our children hung around a bunch of adults either!

4) Don't do it by yourself - Develop a system where all the laundering, cooking, housework and yard work is shared by every family member. We all have a responsibility for the needs of the family. That burden should not fall on just one family member. Don't hesitate to ask for help when you need it.

Finally, whatever it takes to share additional time with them please do it. Whether it is playing dolls, braiding hair, playing catch, going for walks or just sitting and talking. Use this time wisely. You will be learning so many valuable things about your children. Take it from me, you'll need to call upon these parent-child connections in the future.

FOUR

THE WORM AND
THE EARLY BIRD

Education is an important element in the struggle for human rights.
It is the means to help our children and people rediscover
their identity and there by increase self respect.
Education is our passport to the future for
tomorrow belongs to the people who prepare for it today.

—— Minister El-Hajj Malik El-Shabazz

Summer 1983

I read an article in Parade Magazine and was hit by a bolt of inspiration. "That's it!" I exclaimed to Sonja. "Let's forget about the regular school system with those overwhelmed, burned out teachers! Forget about all those street gangs and that negative peer pressure. Let's take 'em out of all of that stuff!" I was already fuming behind published editorials in both the Seattle Times and the Seattle Post Intelligencer newspapers that spoke negatively of non-white academic achievement on recent student (CAT) California Achievement Tests scores.

We were extremely disturbed by the negative implications of those articles because our children were out-performing ninety percent of all children being tested. As a result, they had been placed in something called the 'Horizon Program' for gifted children.

Although we knew ours were not gifted academically, we did

43

The Teacher In Every Parent

know that they were razor sharp. We had prepared their minds in that fashion. We also were aware of many children of color who were scoring high on these tests and achieving positive results in the classroom. According to the newspaper article however, there was very little few Latino, Native American and African American academic achievements. We were keeping our children on the right academic track, but felt that the same broad editorial brush was painting all of us. I wanted to do something about it. The best I could do though was to write a scathing rebuttal and continue to motivate our two kids toward success.

My excitement stemmed from Thomas and Anita Rogers who were the proud parents of three adult children. As with most parents, they would have been proud of their children under most any circumstance. What made them beam the brightest was the academic success of their children. The three Rogers children were exceptional in that each attended an Ivy League College, and none had spent a single day in a formal school setting!

Mrs. Rogers, with no prior teaching experience, decided she could do at least as good a job-if not a superior-to the one she had witnessed while working as a volunteer tutor in the Denver, Colorado school system. Anita Rogers worked in both the private and public school sectors. During that time she witnessed many children who were just not achieving academically. As a mother with children approaching school age, this was of major concern to her. She decided to home school her kids instead-an alternative educational method that had been receiving a great deal of attention in the early 80's. Of course, this concept was not a new phenomenon in the annals of education, but her achievements were.

In reviewing her own educational accomplishments, she realized that not only did she do a better job of preparing her children for college, but she accomplished it in far less time. Mrs.

44

The Worm And The Early Bird

Rogers conducted family school only three days a week, four hours per day. It allowed time for educational field trips, visits to museums or an occasional trip to the park. By the age of sixteen each of her children had taken the Scholastic Assessment Test (SAT) and the American College Test (ACT) test with their lowest score being twelve hundred-fifty on the SAT and twenty-two on the ACT.

Guideline Number Ten: Parents are TEACHING all the time, whether they know it or not.

Sonja, observing my youthful enthusiasm and not wanting to deflate it completely sarcastically said, "Great idea Joe, I work forty hours a week and you work fifty. Whose going to teach 'em? I got it! I'll teach'em. I have no formal teaching experience. Besides, I could use the time off from work!" At times that woman used to get on my nerves. She was right of course. Neither of us could afford to resign our positions to formally teach our children full time.

Upon further examination of the article, I discovered that Mr. Rogers earned a quarter of million dollars per year as a business executive, freeing his spouse to pursue this educational option. It also enabled her to hire personal math, science and foreign language instructors for the children before they were ten. We were hardly in their income bracket, nor did we have the luxury of time that Anita Rogers had. (We barely made sixty-thousand dollars between us). I concluded on my own that this was not a viable option for our family to pursue. Regardless, I was impressed with her early teaching success and decided to study it, hoping to borrow some secrets to use with my own children who were only seven at the time.

When asked about her accomplishments and those of her

The Teacher In Every Parent

children, Mrs. Roger stated that all her children were bright to begin with. Their main assets, she suggested, were that none suffered from any attitude deficiencies that she determined were critical in their academic development. In the previous school settings, she found many children were not achieving because, early on, their attitudes had been adversely affected: either at home or at school.

She then acknowledged that her children were encouraged to think and solve problems for themselves. She began teaching both methods (positive attitudes and independent thinking) very early with her children, and refined her teaching methods with each child. She also recalled her own childhood experience; sitting in class and being stymied by a problem she found hard to solve on her own. The teacher was busy helping other students and she was left unattended. In this scenario, according to Mrs. Rogers, three possible events could occur:

1) The child could sit patiently and wait for assistance.
2) The child could sit and figure out the problem using his or her own critical thinking.
3) The child could just mentally shut down after a while.

The second event occurred in her case. However, Mrs. Rogers found that with the increased class sizes and social challenges that were accompanying many children to school, many were just turning off. Obviously she didn't want that to happen to her children, but said initially, "All I could give my children at first was all the available time I could summons." With no teaching certification (she later received one) and limited experience, she directly contributed to her children's academic success. She accomplished this by giving them expert attention in a structured, one-on-one setting. Through trial and error she compiled an attitude checklist that her children used until they reached the age of thirteen.

She stressed the importance of doing this in a non—threatening way.

The attitude checklist was devised to be used with children six to seventeen years of age. This is the same checklist that I utilized fifteen years ago on our twins in the hope of learning more about them and releasing their true potential.

CHECKLIST FOR CHILD ATTITUDES

Code: 0 =Never • I = Rarely • 2 = Sometimes
3 = Often • 4 = Always

I like challenges.

It's important that I do well in school.

I enjoy finding and correcting my mistakes.

I believe that I can do a good job if I want to.

I can do good work even if I am not very excited about the project.

I like to test myself to find out how good I am.

I can handle setbacks.

I learn from mistakes and try not to make the same mistakes again.

I am willing to accept help when I am stuck or confused.

I believe that my friends respect me.

I believe that my teachers respect me.

I believe that my parents respect me.

People think that I am a hard worker.

I like school.

I finish projects that I start.

I think I am smart.

I enjoy getting good grades.

I enjoy developing my skills and talents,
I enjoy finding solutions to problems.
I am not afraid to take risk and try something difficult.

Once this information was compiled you should discuss their statements and responses with them. Explain the pattern of O's, 1's, and 2's that suggest perhaps some additional work is needed in certain areas to develop a more positive attitude. Let your child know that their opinions are very important. Use common sense when working this checklist because, of course, you know your child better than anyone else. If you don't, you should!

The goal of this attitude checklist is to provide a bench mark to encourage our children to think about achieving and maintaining a great attitude. Things will not always go their way in life. Furthermore in our utilizing this checklist, Mrs. Rogers and I achieved these three main objectives:

1) We provided our children with an opportunity to practice creative problem solving.
2) We encouraged our children to develop their ingenuity.
3) We showed our children how to increase their Smartness Quotient.

From this I later developed a game of 'Cause and Effect' that we played with our children to maintain a closeness and to teach them the responsibility of their actions.

ATTITUDES THAT DEFEAT INTELLIGENCE

There are some powerful elements that compel individuals to protect themselves from weakness, insecurities and vulnerabilities. They generally manifest themselves in the form of

The Worm And The Early Bird

emotional or psychological actions. Children are no exception to these feelings. Children who perceive any physical or intellectual limitations sometimes show one of these four response options:

1) They can deny they have a limitation.
2) They can accept their limitation and resign themselves to it.
3) They can compensate for the limitation by creating alternative methods for attaining their desired objectives. (Clowning around or negative, aggressive behavior)
4) They can avoid confronting the situation that makes them feel inadequate. (denial)

There maybe other responses. However, these are some of the consequences that can prevent our children from accomplishing their goals. Objectives that we all know they are capable of achieving. In a desire to insulate themselves from their frustrations and failures, children sometimes develop distorted perceptions of themselves that can greatly affect their behavior.

For example, Joseph, to our knowledge, was never told by his teacher that he couldn't read while in the first grade. However, he was treated as if he couldn't read even though he was capable. He easily could have accepted the limitations projected on him, and for a short time he did. We all know that a child's perception of his or her abilities greatly influences the goals that they set for themselves. Conscious or unconscious signs given by teachers, parents or other influential authority figures inevitably affect those attitudes. When parents are not involved, that negativity can increase. Had we not interceded on the teacher's diagnosis of our child, he may have been turned off by reading completely.

From that experience I learned that a child's perception of reality, however inaccurate, is still that child's reality. Depending on the circumstances, a child may choose to compensate for a deficiency by becoming the class clown or by causing any number of disruptive acts in class that will allow him to be removed from an environment that he finds uncomfortable. People like Eddie Murphy and Robin Williams have parlayed clownish classroom behavior into stand-up comedy routines and stellar movie careers. In later interviews, they both said they clowned around as a way to compensate for not being equipped to compete in the classroom. I definitely can relate to their rationale, however, many of us who act up in class usually have nothing to look forward to but a date in the principal's office!

Whether this behavior is considered smart or not, I don't know, what I do know is this is evasive action on their part. Unfortunately, if the dilemma isn't confronted on some level by a counselor, parent, teacher or mentor, the situation will generally escalate later in adult life. Students who struggle in math during elementary school for example, may decide to never take another math course once their math requirements are fulfilled. Furthermore, as adults they may delegate the family checkbook or other responsibilities for paying bills to their spouse or shy away from any employment possibilities that require the use of math.

I knew a guy who didn't read, not because he couldn't read but because he was told that he was 'slow' reader by a teacher. That awareness created a vulnerability that magnified his alleged inadequacy. It had a negative effect on both his self confidence and self-esteem. It also killed his potential to develop a love of reading.

As parents we can help eliminate most of this negativity in our children by first identifying, then redirecting these self defeating thoughts. We also can add to their self esteem by addressing them only in a positive manner. Which means we must work on our own issues and not take the problems of our day out on our children! By doing this early and consistently, we can develop and

The Worm And The Early Bird

nurture smart children who feel they have worth in tomorrow's world.

We used to simply call our children VIPs (Very Important People) all the time regardless of the situation-Especially when they had done something inappropriate. For example, anytime our children did anything they were not supposed to be doing, one of us would say: "I can't believe you would do that because you are a VIP, and VERY IMPORTANT PEOPLE don't do things like that." Sounds and is simple........It also is very effective!
We found this basic technique would quickly redirect them back into the positive attitude mode.

I discovered that the positive attitude mode was crucial. This was done by effectively having them concentrate on what they were capable of doing, rather than what they had already done. This made them become smarter children by helping them utilize their developing skills to make better judgments, get better grades in school, and become leaders in everything they attempted. In time, it also convinced us that our children were mature, responsible and deserved more freedom. You can't imagine how gratifying it was to see them using their talents in a positive, constructive manner, rather than on some negative or self defeating behavior.

Once we learned how to effectively do this, we stopped spanking our children. Something that really wasn't working anyway. Corporal punishment, something that many of us grew up with, really was, and is done because a parent has generally lost control of their child. (Most of us have found ourselves there.) I found that using the VIP method not only increased their capabilities, it also enabled them to train themselves to achieve practically anything they wanted later in life. They began writing down and focusing on their goals!

Developing smart thinking skills in adults or children is similar to developing strong, hard muscles in our bodies. If you don't continue to exercise them, our muscles will get soft and atrophy. However, when utilized on a daily basis, they get rock hard and increase in size. These smart thinking skills are desperately needed because children and adults will surely encounter challenges in life. It is impossible to live in this world and not have obstacles to overcome.

As author Charles Swindoll says, "I am convinced that life is ten percent what happens to me and ninety percent how I react to it." Smart thinking children will have a distinct advantage over other children. They will find a way to overcome these obstacles faster and more effectively. We must overcome these disadvantages because as we know, in America, jails are being constructed faster than school houses. Unfortunately, in the years to come, many of our children will find their way into these institutions. They also never will be reformed by these periods of incarceration. This tragic political plight levied against our young people can be alleviated only if we take control of our childrens futures back.

Another challenge facing us is the fact that one in five children in this country lives in poverty. Most of these kids are neglected by overburdened, worn down parents. Many parents are not equipped to handled their own lives, much less the lives of their children, on a mental, emotional or spiritual level. We can't afford to allow any child to turn off on education because when that occurs, they also lose an opportunity for that slice of the American dream. They deserve to live a good life as an adult, however the preparation for it starts today! So if life gets hard for us adults, we need to get tough, dig in and go forward anyway! Our kids deserve it. The renowned minister Robert Schuller says, "People do not plan to fail, but they fail to plan." Plan, push, try and never, ever give up.

FIVE

NETWORKING

*The best portion of a good man's life are his little, nameless,
unremembered acts of kindness and of love.*

—Wordsworth

Spring 1984

Our children loved participating in athletics while they
were growing up. They found a comfortable place in sports
because it taught them how to compete and handle temporary
setbacks and losses. They also developed lifelong friendships
through their activities. They skied, played soccer, basketball,
football, baseball and ran track. We received much satisfaction
from these activities primarily because it was what they enjoyed
doing, although these extra curricular duties kept us hopping!

Of all the activities, the sport that gave us the most pleasure
was track and field. This was usually an all day occurrence that
started the third Saturday in May and concluded the second week
in August. What we enjoyed the most was that track brought all
family members out. Everybody participated in consoling the
youngsters who hadn't done as well as they had hoped,
congratulated the ones who were successful, and encouraged
them all to practice harder to improve their performances. All the
parents and relatives would pack huge meals and share them with
each other. They also would share rides. We started at ten o'clock
in the morning and wouldn't conclude until six o'clock in the
evening.

The Teacher In Every Parent

This camaraderie was especially appreciated by most parents because Saturday was probably the only day they could sleep in--Although we never did. It was while attending these SCAA (South Central Athletic Association) track and field meets that we learned the concept of networking. We had to because we had spread ourselves too thin. In our quest to provide the very best for our children, we had become fast paced taxi cabs. Sonja would have Jawanna, and I would have Joseph. Occasionally, we would meet the middle, exchange greetings and be on our way. This was through out the week, as well as on weekends.

For a brief period in the spring and fall of 1984, our Saturdays typically went like this: Joseph had tennis practice from 5:30-7:00 am. Then a shower, breakfast and into his football gear for a 9:00 game. From there, it was home for a shower, lunch and a 1:00 PM soccer game. Then from 4:30-5:30 it was clarinet lessons. For Jawanna's part, her activities included a basketball game at 9:00 am, home for lunch, followed by a track event at 1:00 p.m. to approximately 3:30, and clarinet practice from 4:30-5:30!

At the time, what we were doing didn't have all the organization and sophistication of today's networking systems, however, it worked much the same. Although this idea was new to me, it didn't change the fact that this system had been around for hundreds of years.

In biblical times this combination of bartering or networking was the primary form of doing business. If you had a talent or skill you could exchange it for something you required, rather than paying with currency. When paying their tithes and offering, many parishioners would give their ten percent in goods or services,

For example, if there was a local Blacksmith in town, he would generally provide the shoeing for all horses in exchange for whatever goods and services he required. I used to be a pretty fair

54

Networking

barber and would often exchange that service for the services of my friends who were skilled in yard work and auto mechanics. Concerning this and many other subjects, one man that I admire immensely is Luke McCray. He was a mentor of mine who taught me a great deal about networking through sharing his advanced knowledge of Track and Field. Luke was a nurse and a tireless worker whose kids all excelled in track and field. As a young parent, I learned from him the importance of our children becoming self-disciplined and trained. He once told me that, "Running is one of best ways to condition an athlete's mind, body and spirit." He explained to me that once trained, an athlete can accomplish any academic task as well.

As I discovered through my own children, he was absolutely correct. From then on my baseball teams were the best conditioned in the city, and our record of achievements backed that up. For my part of the networking and bartering contract, I helped Luke understand the nuances of the game of baseball. It was also a sport that his son, David had a great deal of ability in. However, David was far too accomplished in the area of track and field to give up that sport. Unfortunately for Luke, he was so experienced in practically everything, there wasn't anything I could do to assist him with. Most of the time I just sat there and soaked all of his life experience in.

Guideline Number Eleven: Help another child whenever you can: Yours will be the beneficiary.

Normally, one of the working parents has some flexibility in their working schedules that can allow them to assist other parents for certain activities. This bartering and networking plan can work well when each parent provides a service. Sonja had working schedule that was not flexible. However, being in real

The Teacher In Every Parent

estate at the time, my schedule was more allowing.

What I learned was that in networking, everyone has a skill to offer. Something of value that they can contribute. Of course, at times, it must first be identified. The first strategy in making networking a successful experience is to attend the initial orientation of any activity. By doing this you will have an opportunity to meet with the teachers, coaches or instructors involved. They will usually know how to plug you into the networking system. Second, this is your opportunity to meet all of the parents and identify which ones are involved in the car pooling phase of the networking system. This is the primary concern for most parents. In these meetings it's important to be as open minded, friendly, and extroverted as possible. Moreover, be prepared to do something to reciprocate at some point in time.

In the beginning, I usually found myself transporting two or three additional children with me to the activities of our children. We were going there anyway and the parents were obviously appreciative of our efforts. My only concern was getting some parents to respond in kind. Surprisingly, some parents try to pass their children off on you! I easily corrected that by asking these parents to identify their strengths so the group could utilize them. It was the only way to avoid a one sided situation.

As a result of our children's involvement in team sports, ballet, and gymnastics, we expanded our networking to receive group rates on plays, museum visits, even the movies. Our love for whatever they desired to do was the driving force in our continuing to involve ourselves. I bartered by volunteering to coach two recreational league basketball teams and car pooling children around while Sonja excelled at organizing parents to buy trophies for season-ending parties and after event treats. Through her efforts, I was exclusively free to coach and mentor young people, something I was very passionate about.

Networking

I enjoyed coaching because through sports I was able to positively influence the lives of many children. This was done by teaching them the relevance of discipline, planning, and goal setting in other areas of their lives. In this way I was sharing my love of sports, children and teaching with others as well as benefiting from their talents and skills in the process.

I also wanted to encourage other parents to use this time to bond more with their children by doing the same thing. What I discovered was that not all parents were as actively involved with their children to the degree that we were. I don't think we were overzealous. We merely enjoyed being with them and watching their development. Quite frankly, I was secretly troubled by these parents, but attempted to be understanding. Everybody has something they are working to get better at. I felt inspired to help them learn how to share in the precious lives of their own children.

There are several factors that can impede the development of this bonding—being in a job or career that has an inflexible work schedule, as stated earlier, can slice into the time necessary for togetherness to occur. Another factor is being a single or secondary parent. (this includes guardians, god-parents, boy friends or girl friends) It's difficult for a busy single parent to partake in all of the activities of their child. However, secondary and single parents need to attempt to attend at least some of their child's activities. It is necessary for us to keep our children involved in activities and away from idle time, so it is imperative that we attempt networking. I believe the ones who have the most parenting success, barter and network with each other on a regular basis.

At times I found that some parents use the circumstances of their lives as an occasional excuse for not attending the recital, play, or a ball game. In our circle, there was always one parent

The Teacher In Every Parent

who made excuses and would successfully manipulate the other parents into handling many of her parenting responsibilities.

Once I taught tennis to a woman's son for next to nothing because he was a talented, well behaved and mannerly youngster. I really didn't mind initially, however, there came a time when I insisted that she at least attend one of his tournaments. After all nobody is that busy! Through several conversations with her, I discovered that she enjoyed baking, and from then on, she became our designated dessert maker for any activity her son participated in. She really had a great time because finally she was contributing something to the simple networking and bartering structure.

As I would meet with some of these parents, I was completely amazed by how much drugs and drug abuse had devastated their families. Even mothers, who were generally the backbones of most families had fallen victim to the street drug called 'crack cocaine.' This was a cheaper, more concentrated version of cocaine or coke. Cocaine is classified as a narcotic, although its general effect on the body is stimulating more than depressing. The drug reached its apex during the disco days of the late seventies and early eighties. It had begun a comeback in the late eighties and early to mid nineties. Today however, crack cocaine generally rules the inner city streets of most cities; destroying families and ruining lives. Some inventive chemist devised a method to take this drug a step further. In a more concentrated form coke is not "snorted" but "smoked." By smoking the drug, the "high" apparently is more intense because the drug gets into the bloodstream more rapidly. The high however is quick, short and highly addicting.

In this yellowy, waxy, concentrated form, this drug is cheaper to produce as well. The result is that it's also very inexpensive causing more people to get hooked quicker. I've met people who will sell their first born for this drug. It has generally made slaves out of many who have used it. If you ever notice this, or any drug in the possession of your young people, do something to interseed quickly. This drug and many others are killing communities all over this country.

It was extremely difficult to network with many of these parents on behalf of their children. You almost have to adopt the kid! As parents, we have to be better than this. We must become more DISCIPLINED. We need to become stronger parents in order to lead our children. Nancy Reagan said simply, 'Say No To Drugs.' With all respect, the former first lady doesn't quite get it. Besides just saying "No" you must have something to say yes to. We need to say YES to something, and that something is the positive future of our children. Dare to be unique. Dare to set a good example. Dare to be a great parent and role model!

DARE

Dare to be different
when all around you seek conformity.

Dare to encounter obstacles
when all around you avoid conflict.

Dare to seek possibilities
when all around you see only the impossible.

Dare to seek new and greater challenges
when all around you are procrastinating.

Dare to remain strong
when all around you are weakening.

Dare to continue
when all around you are quitting.

Dare to have faith
when all around you are doubting.

Dare to dream
even if no one dreams with you.

SIX

FAMILY MEETINGS

Talking is a digestive process which is absolutely essential
to the mental constitution of the man who devours many books.
A full mind must have talk, or it will grow stagnate.
The first ingredient in conversation is truth, the next is good sense,
the third, good humor, and the fourth is wit.

—Sir William Temple

Summer 1985

Like many homes in my neighborhood my mother ran the show. We complied with her house rules (they were rules, not guidelines) or we found a new place to live—Something I once did for about four days! There was little recourse, and change wasn't going to occur unless she wanted it to. Until I became a parent, I remember saying, "Just wait until I'm grown. I'm going to let my kids do anything they want to!" Of course that was in response to not getting what I wanted at the time. **I repeat, that was before I became a parent!** This situation isn't any good for children and can really drive parents crazy.

In discussing family meetings as a component in developing well-balanced children and maintaining family unity, a couple of misconceptions need to be cleared up. First of all, family meetings were beneficial for our family because in the beginning, I had a know it all, dictator type personality. That's OK if you live the life of a hermit, however, that won't cut it in a family environment.

The Teacher In Every Parent

You see, I had begun to run my house precisely like the one I was raised in. Although that strategy was working, nobody was really happy but me.

In the beginning that's all I knew. However, once we discovered family meetings, we began to look forward to them and even made lists of the topics that would be discussed in future meetings.

The meetings taught me the importance of the opinions of others and the sharing of ideas, which is crucial in making a house really a home. It's also a place where children function the most efficiently.

When some of our married friends were experiencing trouble communicating with their children and asked why we weren't having the same problems. I assured them that we did. We just kept those challenges to a minimum through the use of our newly acquired family meetings. We saw these meetings as an opportunity to encourage our children to be involved in their family. When I said this, I knew that many of my friends already felt overwhelmed. They saw this as yet something else they needed to add to their already busy schedules. As a result, most of our friends were reluctant to discuss the idea of a family meeting with me, much less put anything regarding it into practice. Where the negative feelings originated regarding family meetings is anybody's guess. Since I didn't have such meetings in my home when I was a child, I was at a loss to explain why they felt that way. I knew that some of today's parents were either too busy or had a bad childhood experience with family meetings to investigate them further. After all family meetings, like most things relating to our homes, were around a lot longer than I have been. I also discovered that change is tough for many people.

Although these concerns are valid, my experience has taught me that if parents can get over their own fears, (False Elusions

Family Meetings

Appearing Real), they will find these meetings quiet helpful.

I figured if I could get over living in a dictatorship, they could get over their own anxieties as well. I continued by informing them that this special time served as an excellent tool for us in resolving conflicts before they got out of control. When I was growing up, I heard that fighting was a natural way of releasing tension and clearing the air. This obviously was an untrue statement because fights of any kind, end with hurt and miserable feelings afterwards. We have all seen volatile situations brewing and did or said nothing about them. We may have even discounted them as a temporary phase. However, I never wanted to take the risk of not communicating and having bad feelings come out later.

These family sessions also provided an opportunity for everyone to speak and be heard without being judged. They allowed children to feel like part of the process when planning general house business. Our children learned in a safe environment, that their voice counted. In time they grew more intelligent and became more extroverted children. They also benefited by acquiring better decision making skills while working in the family group. These are very important skills that can be carried into adulthood.

We learned that with regular practice in this environment, our children developed self confidence as well. Parents will also benefit by learning how to acquire and maintain high standards for their kids. They will learn how to delegate responsibilities and authority too! In this way there is no reason to attempt super-human feats, burning themselves out in the processes.

Communication is increased and just as importantly, parents tend to set better examples because they will normally have their children's undivided attention. This is where we can truly become role models for our children. It saddens me when I hear kids speak of athletics and rock stars as role models. These people

The Teacher In Every Parent

should be individuals whose talents we admire, not people we want to emulate completely. First of all, we know very little about them personally.

Although I enjoy watching him play the game, I lost some respect for Michael Jordan, the basketball great from the Chicago Bulls in the Mid 80's. This was the time when practically every kid in America wanted a pair of Air Nike basketball shoes. My boy included. During this same time however, some misguided ones were approaching other kids, beating or killing them, and taking their shoes. Imagine, killing someone in the name of a pair shoes.

The prices of these shoes were thought to be at the center of the problem. They were over one hundred dollars a pair! Many individuals knew that Jordan had the most influence with the people running the Nike corporation. Many felt he also had a responsibility to attempt to reduce the price of these sneakers. This would make them more accessible to people, which might stop some of the violence. When asked his thoughts concerning this, his response was, "It's unfortunate that kids are hurting each other for Nike shoes. However, I don't feel that I should bear the responsibility for this solely. I do feel that something can be worked out." Spoken like a true marketer. Nothing, at least price-wise, was ever worked out and kids continued to die.

Even though he was a young man and still coming to grips with his mega stardom, I was nevertheless disappointed with his point of view. Nobody was asking him to solely take on that responsibility. Just acknowledge the fact both you and the company you represent have a responsibility to the communities you sell to. Besides, you had both lined your pockets sufficiently during this time. It appeared as though Mike had come from a good family so I guess I just expected more from him. I bet now that he has children he thinks differently! Anyway the violence caused by greed for designer shoes slowly shifted when another lure, drugs, was dropped into the marketplace: Drugs.....Personal commentary over. Now back to family meetings.

It's amazing how children respond when they witness their family working together to plan, and organize activities or to resolve conflicts. Our kids were inspired and more likely to share their concerns as they arose. (And those concerns did come). Many use this time to discuss and plan everything from daily household duties to family vacations and day trips.

Cooking was a dilemma that had to be worked out in our home. Here's what we did. When it was time to prepare a meal, for example, everybody found something constructive to do to lighten the burden on Sonja. One of us would set the table, one would make the salad, while another would help prepare the meal. We shared every chore from dishwashing to yard work. In our family meetings it was agreed that no gender stereotypes would exist. As our lives intertwined we would help each other as much as possible. We would help them with their homework and they would assist us in our work related projects.

As I learned later from discussion with our children, they really looked forward to having something to do during this time because it made them feel important and involved. If we were all working hard, and smart enough to accomplish our goals, success will follow!

Guideline Number Twelve: Encourage everyone in your family to participate in order for all to benefit.

In my experience with these meetings, I was most gratified by the promotion of family unity and teamwork that came from them. Our attitude checklist was introduced during these family meetings, which had a dynamic affect on everyone in our family (especially our children). The style of these get togethers can be

The Teacher In Every Parent

like your family in general; they can be structured and regimented or relaxed and low-keyed. These guidelines can vary in your family depending on what direction your family chooses to go. That is the only decision that is totally up to the parents or guardians.

Through interviewing parents who did incorporate family meetings, I realized that there were several types of parents raising children. Some came from strict homes, some came from liberal households, and I discovered no consistent fallout as a result. Many parents from tightly run homes conducted their homes in much the same manner. Some rebelled totally from that rigidly conducted family structure. Many parents from loosely run homes ran a surprisingly tight ship. Still many liberal parents raise their children in their own image. Some follow the pattern set and some rejected it, however, most agreed that allowing their children to do almost anything they wanted could create problems later. Whatever type of parent we happen to be, total family involvement is a necessary component for maximum benefit.

Even though we are the parents and have the financial responsibility (we pay the bills), the home actually belongs to everyone. We all have a role to play. Through our family meetings it was agreed that everyone would involve themselves in doing their share to keep the house in good working order. The most important component for these meetings is that they be quick, concise, consistent and have an agenda. We initially needed a formal setting to show the importance of what we were attempting to do. (Otherwise, our children would have thought it was another game!) It was conducted similar to an official board meeting. We met weekly, usually on Saturday mornings following breakfast. Yours meetings can be monthly, bi-monthly or weekly, but there needs to be consistency to reach the desired effect.

In the beginning our meetings lasted no longer than fifteen

minutes and generally covered topics such as chores, homework, day trips, what television shows were to be video taped for the week. (There was no TV during the week.) We also discussed any disagreements that may have occurred since the last meeting. Any topic should be open for discussion provided that it's relevant to the family. In our family, anybody could hold an emergency family meeting at anytime.

In families where there are older adolescents, everyone should make an effort to attend these meetings. Extremely busy family members need to understand that these times will, in many cases, be one of few opportunities your group will have to come together as a family unit. The more commitment any family has, the greater the outcome of these family meetings will be.

Treating this time with respect is crucial, especially when determining dates. Insisting that family meetings be mandatory is an excellent strategy that should be enforced when necessary.

Guideline Number Thirteen: Always put your family members before anything—including your friends.

During the meetings hit all your topics hard, fast, and with a sense of humor. All decisions should be decided by general agreement. (Voting) (Be aware that at times children will side with each other or genders will merge to gain an advantage!) There were four in our family and frequently we would be deadlocked. In the event of a tie, a coin flip would always decide it. Children will quickly discover that heads comes approximately 70% of the time.

Finally, you should always find time in the meetings to acknowledge any accomplishments of a family member. Again, this reinforces an atmosphere of family unity. Attaining honor roll status, sports honors, attaining professional licenses, or job promotions were all excuses for us to call attention to and celebrate with our family members. Between meetings we always posted an update board that was accessible to everyone. Again, run your house like you would run a business!

However, from time to time the subject of allowances would come up. It was one of the few topics that was not open for negotiation. My opinion on the subject was, why reward a child monetarily for something, that if introduced correctly, they would feel honored to do.

Besides, there were always other opportunities to earn a dollar or two. In fact, in many cases we would just arbitrarily give them five or ten dollars for a job well done. I just didn't believe in being obligated to do so!

As young parents, we agreed that in our home the number one responsibility was the care of our children. They hadn't asked to be born into this world, and the fact that we were young and careless was no excuse. The least we could do was to provide them as much as was humanly possible. Much of our income was spent on their education. A very worthwhile place for our finances, I thought. For their part, the children's number one responsibility was to have pride in themselves and to excel in everything they attempted. Their mother would always say, "I don't ask much of you two. I just want you to give me everything you have to give." I believed in that philosophy because, sick or well, that is precisely what she gave and continues to give them. Their second responsibility was to have respect and love for others. That may sound vague and superficial but many negative actions of young people are brought about by inferiority complexes, low self esteem and a lack of respect for others.

Family Meetings

SOME WAYS TO INCREASE YOUR CHILD'S SELF ESTEEM ARE:

1) Connection -Show your child how you really feel about them. Nothing works better than a wink, a smile, hug, gentle pats of praise or some playful wrestling. Tell them things like, "I think you're fantastic!" or "I love you very much." Don't be afraid to share your ideas, experiences and hobbies with them because sharing teaches closeness.

2) Power -Encourage your child to think independently. Allow them to experience first hand, the consequences of their actions. Provide opportunities and skills to help them learn to solve problems. Don't be in a hurry to do everything for them. If they are anything like us, 'The cream will rise to the top.'

3) Modeling - Set the best possible example for your child. Before doing anything ask yourself, "Is this something that my family will be proud of me for doing?" Showing is always better than telling anyway! Help your child understand what he believes by being crystal clear about what your family values are.

4) Individuality - Encourage your child to express ideas that may not be the same as yours. Show them they are special by trying to look at the world through their eyes. Let them know that it's perfectly OK to be different and not follow the crowd.

SEVEN

THE NEGATIVE POWER OF TELEVISION

It is impossible to make people understand their ignorance,
for it requires knowledge to perceive it.

—Jeremy Taylor

Autumn 1985

Sonja wasn't a big fan of television sets in the home. She thought they detracted from the decor of any room. I'm not aware of when her dislike of televisions started, but I do know she did not always have it. As an adolescent, she used to monopolize her family's only tube by telling her mother she needed to watch certain TV shows for school assignments! Now that is an original lie. Although I can't believe her brothers and sisters were ever fooled by that scam.

I didn't watch a great deal of TV as a child, but I enjoyed my share. My mother had little tolerance for what she called 'TV Crazy Kids,' therefore our television watching was well below the national average. Besides, my brothers and I were more doers than watchers. We liked participating rather than being entertained. Growing up, I was a very competitive athlete, excelling in baseball, football, and cross country running. This left little time for any real dedicated television watching.

In the beginning, I enjoyed playing chess more than playing sports. On any given weekend, I could have easily been found at

The Negative Power Of Television

Rotary's Boy's and Girl's club, where bi-monthly chess tournaments were held. I won my share of trophies too. When we did watch TV, the fact that I hadn't grown up in a traditional family setting acutely affected the type of television I was attracted to. (Which explains why I don't watch much these days.) As a child I loved shows such as Leave it to Beaver, Father Knows Best, Bewitched, The Donna Reed Show, My Three Sons, The Dick Van Dyke Show and The Honeymooners, to name just few.

As I explored my thoughts on the subject, I discovered that I enjoyed these shows so much because there was always a male influence in these TV homes and there was always a sense of sharing—whether real or imagined. These men all seemed to have a compassionate side to them, and growing up, I longed to have a strong, understanding male in my life. Some shows, like Bewitched also had a make believe side to them. A person was made to believe that he could just 'twitch his nose' and change his circumstances!

I never blamed anyone for the circumstances in my life and always attempted to achieve in spite of some of the disadvantages. Having a mother like mine in our lives was quite an advantage anyway. Until she remarried, she alone was routinely responsible for motivating us with one of her southern spun stories of achievement. Since we all desired to please her in whatever way possible, we generally did everything to make her life as pleasant as we possibly could—although we had our moments! We tried with such vigor to make her happy because we saw the daily sacrifices she made for us. The fact that she didn't like us watching a lot television was just another thing we attempted to do to satisfy our mom. Besides, her stories were much better.

As parents, Sonja and I monitored and minimized all television viewing. Outside of our home was another matter however. Every time Joseph would spend the night at a friend's house, he would come home with some new term or crazy maneuver that had to be dislodged from his personality; something I would gladly do. When break dancing was very popular in early 80's, he returned once from an overnighter with his shoes intentionally unlaced and his pants hanging off his midriff. They had adopted this look from watching some television show the previous night. Observing this new style I inquired, "What do you call that look Joe?" "I'm saggin," he responded with authority. He said it was suave and that everybody was doing it. I asked him to get me something from the refrigerator. When he got up and began to walk, I stepped on his shoestring, causing him to stumble. When he got up I said, "This is the Smith house and we don't walk around looking like idiots. Don't let me see that look again. Besides, you're a VIP. He got the message. We never saw that look again.

Guideline Number Fourteen: If it looks like duck and walks like a duck, it could be a mixed up child. Stop and inquire.

In watching television I also noticed that many problems were solved in half-hour intervals. Amazing as it sounds, some children start to believe that these sit-coms are quick fix methods to the problems they face. This is especially played out today when children don't get the instant results they desire and sometimes resort to hostile methods. Sometimes they take their frustrations out by victimizing another child. Our use of the VCR and a little planning insured that the best viewing with (less commercials) could be achieved.

Television has changed dramatically from the time that I was a child. I'm not sure if my views are a manifestation of just getting older and becoming more sentimental, or if TV has actually

The Negative Power Of Television

become more graphic and violent over time. At times it's easy to reminisce about better times and diminish anything new as too racy as we get on in years. There's an old saying that I find myself using more often as I approach forty. It says simply, "The older I get, the better I was." As time moves forward for us, we occasionally modify this to say, 'Things were much better back in the good old days.' Even with all of my rationalizing, I do believe that overall today's television has taken a turn for the worst. There seems to be a new style in the media that takes far more risks in the development of their story lines.

They truly have become more graphic and violent in nature.This was a serious departure from even the 1960's TV shows that were considered too graphic at the time. It also has been some radical change from the wholesome, family oriented shows that I grew up with.

When television was first created and introduced to the public in 1939, it was designed as an entertainment vehicle that someday could be utilized in every home. That goal has been realized with almost all American households (99 %) having at least one television set. (Parke & Slaby 1995)

Overall however, the quality of shows being created today has diminished. Television producers, in an attempt to find that multi-million dollar hit show, will usually churn out hundreds of situation comedies or dramatic movie pilots every year. Of course not all of these shows make it off the producer's cutting floor and on to our television sets, but enough of these garbage shows hit the air waves every television season. Watching this medium on a regular basis can have a negative affect on whoever watches it. That should be a concern to any parent who wants the absolute best for their child.

Many of our children spend more time watching television than they do attending school—on average forty to fifty hours

The Teacher In Every Parent

per week. This total is generally higher for non-white children. Part of the problem is that parents usually don't feel that excessive television viewing has any adverse effect on their child's general upbringing, therefore they have little problem with their viewing habits. It is important to realize that television watching usually encourages passivity, not creativity.

Marie Winn, in The Plug-in Drug, suggests that passivity and inactivity are induced more by the single act of watching television than anything else. She claims that persons watching excessive television become physically relaxed, almost trance-like in their behavior. Also in this "narcotized" state, people often develop withdrawal symptoms that include grouchiness and restlessness. I also discovered that television watching is generally considered a major obstacle in language development as well. According to Dr. Elaine McEwan, author of Super Child, television watching inhibits talking in the early school years and can sometimes create withdrawn, introverted children. The reason for this that most television watching is not interactive and can sometimes stunt a child's verbal growth. Children generally watch TV, and are entertained without having to get involved or be challenged. To further illustrate this point Ann Landers, published this anonymous poem:

TeeVee
In the house
Of Mr. and Mrs. Spouse
He and she
Would watch TeeVee,
And never a word
Between them was spoken
Until the day

The Negative Power Of Television

The set was broken
Then, "How do you do?"
Said He to She
" I don't believe we've met
Spouse is my name.
What's yours?" he asked.
"Why mine is the same"
Said She to He.
"Do you suppose we could be...?"

Excessive television viewing also can limit a child's physical development. Running, hopping, jumping, skipping, and other forms play are essential elements in creating and maintaining a child's overall health. Today in America, almost twenty million youngsters are involved in some kind of sport. Exercise and sports provide our children an opportunity to make friends, build confidence as well as self-esteem. Language enhancement is obviously a major component in a preschooler's overall development in their preparation for mainstream school. Unfortunately excessive TV viewing normally encourages inactivity in most people.

In my experience as a coach, I found that active kids also developed a sense of autonomy, self discipline and good sportsmanship. However my main discovery was that these athletics, whatever their age, were kids who became positive leaders. They also were not afraid of taking risks. I am troubled by reductions in funds for physical education programs in the public schools through levies failures.

It also has been well documented that children who are involved in school sports and other school activities normally enjoy better attendance and generally do better academically than children who don't participate. There is also the area of violence in

The Teacher In Every Parent

our society. Nobody will argue with the fact that there has been an increase in crimes of all sorts among our young people today. Juvenile crime has increased 1000% between 1975-1995. Studies have shown a direct correlation between youth violence and excessive television viewing. The amount of violence that continues to be portrayed on television is something that we should be extremely concerned about!

According to the Neilson ratings, seven of the top ten television shows had a violent theme attached to them in 1995. By the age of 16, it's estimated that our children have seen a approximately 13,000 killings on television (Liebert & Schwartzberg, 1977). Many studies have found that watching television violence amplifies any viewers' aggressive behavior. During this same period, it also desensitizes our children to violent behavior over time.

A twenty-year study by Eron & Huesmann found that children who watched six or more hours of television per day, were twice as likely to have a criminal record by the time they turned twenty one. They were also predictably far more violent than other young people in general. It's clear that our children are far more violent and aggressive than they have ever been in the past. Many times they don't know why either! Our children are carrying knives, handguns, and automatic weapons to school on a regular basis, both as protection from others and as perpetrators who reek havoc against their peers. While working in the public school system in 1995, I found and confiscated a handgun from a twelve year old!

We need to become more aware what of excessive television viewing is doing to our children. Witnessing violence on a regular basis also creates a numbing effect on our children as well. Watching what is happening to our young people is tragic and should shock us all to do something about it. We should never use this medium as a baby sitter either, but we do.

The Negative Power Of Television

It's far too lethal a weapon.

Guideline Number Fifteen: If parents believe they should, they can control the amount of television their children watch.

Another problem of mine where television is concerned is the many stereotypes that are developed and perpetuated through constant television watching. For example, women are still seen in subservient roles catering to domineering, powerful men. People of color are many times shown in a negative light as well which can send a subtle, yet powerful message to children and adults alike.

Even the television that call themselves positive family shows are generally nothing more than situation COMEDIES. These are powerful negative messages being conveyed to young impressionable minds. It is clearly about time for these negatives stereotypes disappear. However, knowing they never will totally go away, it's incumbent upon us to take control of this situation and keep television viewing to an extreme minimum.

Along these same lines are the powerful advertising messages that brainwash the minds of our children. Advertisers have been targeting designer clothes, jeans, hats, shoes and games at our children in an attempt to boost their profits. The latest example is the target marketing of special deodorants for young girls in the ten to thirteen age group. Advertisers are extremely talented in the game of market segmentation.

The market segment game that has been targeted lately is the one that can least afford to purchase anything. I call this group the financially challenged! These people don't have great paying jobs. They usually aren't as educated as the population in general either. However like most parents, these folks want the best for

The Teacher In Every Parent

their children. Unlike most however they will usually pay their last dime in an attempt to keep up with the "Jones."

A classic example of items people unknowing get taken advantage of are designer clothing. Many years ago these types of clothing were exclusively for the rich. These clothes were very expensive. The higher the prices, the less available the purchasers. In the last fifteen years however, advertisers have begun showing clothing manufacturers a way to expand their customer base. They decided to mass produce designer clothing to the general public.

Some parents, in an attempt to build, repair or expand a relationship with their child, many times fall victim to these advertising ploys. Some parents choose to inspire their children by purchasing the latest designer items, in an attempt to keep pace with their contemporaries. Realizing this, advertisers decided to market general brand name merchandise at a somewhat lower price. For the average consumer, this represented an opportunity to purchase these designer clothes and emulate the rich. They enjoyed the privilege of prancing around with the manufacturers' name emblazoned across their chest or hips. Of course the prices of these brand name articles were, in many cases, twice as much as the prices they were previously paying. Conclusion: Today these items are so abundant that misinformed people are actually purchasing basic brand name merchandise at designer prices! The latest targets are our children through games and movies. We have to become parents who are more aware! We have been fooled long enough by sly, aggressive, advertising.

As a result of this marketing, according to Teenage Research Unlimited, American teenagers spent one hundred-ninety million dollars on clothing and entertainment in 1995. Nearly half (46%) of those polled listed parents and occasional jobs, as the source of this income. Next came regular allowance, (29%), part time jobs.

The Negative Power Of Television

and full time jobs (11%). Much of this total was funded by parents and most was spent because of slick advertising. We have to stop being suckers!

Obviously I'm not implying that there is no good that can come from television viewing. I do feel however that what is viewed is as important as how much we view it. There are some great educational shows on television such as Sesame Street, Electric Company and Nickelodeon to name a few.

I enjoy these shows because they provide for interactive viewing rather than the passive variety. There are some very good television programs on public broadcast channels and if one was so inclined, they could create their own thirty minute television show on the public access network. I love a well written movie with a great plot. I also enjoy watching some sports events, as well as national and international news. But I'm not going to waste valuable time watching something I'm not enhanced by.

When our children were around six or seven we gradually began to eliminate television. By the age of nine they were watching edited, video taped TV shows on weekends only. What I realized was that our kids didn't attempt to 'hit us up' for the latest toy or cereal the way our children did. Later they told us that they really didn't miss television. In its place we played games. Lot of games! I was always in love with games. Any kind of game would do as long as it required some thought. The emphasis was on board games. I taught the kids to play checkers, chess, backgammon, dominoes and card games of any kind. They also enjoyed Monopoly and Life. Joseph would always attempt to cheat and we would generally catch him. The focus of the games we played were to instruct the children in the art of thinking. After which a decision was forthcoming. As we know, thinking requires the processing of information. It was our experience that these board games were actually head games. They also learned being smart was cool, not stupid as some young people today believe. It also increased their decision making powers and their smartness.

Once I told a friend that I didn't watch much TV. He responded with, "What are you, some kind of walking intellectual?" I assured them that I'm not even in that time zone. However, why is it that if a guy enjoys reading a book or two, he has to be an intellectual? Just a thought. I prefer a good book to a television show any day of the week.

Whenever possible we should watch TV with our children. Do it first for the pure enjoyment of sharing time with them. Second, there is an opportunity to stimulate thought and conversation with them and to encourage them to watch quality shows—something they will pass on to their children. Television viewing, when utilized properly, can positively promote family relationships by helping to stimulate discussions. It also helps to establish and enhance our children's decision making qualities.

EIGHT

THE POWER SHIFT

In all the trade of war no feat is nobler than a brave retreat.

—Thomas Bittler

July 2, 1986

I attended my first hockey game when I was thirteen years old. The game was played at the old Seattle Center Arena and the Seattle Totems were in rare form that night, winning the game 6-2. I was brand new to the sport of hockey where fist fights seemed to breakout as rapidly as the puck slid across the ice. In fact, that night I learned the phrase, "I went to a fight and a hockey game broke out!" I thought it was rather amusing. During the contest, I repeatedly bugged my friend Christopher Ben regarding every aspect of the happenings that evening: What's the blue line? What's offside? What's high sticking? Where did they learn to skate so well? Why do these guys fight so much? Why are the referees just standing there watching them fight? Finally, how long does that guy have to spend in the penalty box? I don't recall Christopher and I ever going to another hockey game again. I must have asked far too many questions. I have always been the curious type.

Although I never acquired a love for the sport of hockey, from that experience I did recall a term that was frequently used when one team had a skating advantage over the other because of a penalty. Sometimes it's a five-four advantage. Sometimes it's a five-three. It's called a Power play. Later, to fit our home environment, I modified the term to the Power shift.

We experienced our first shift in parent-child power relations on this particular date when Joseph was only ten years old. It was caused of my son's "champagne appetite." Where he acquired this fetish for expensive food and clothing is still a mystery to me. Although through his many athletic associations, he came into contact with children from some very wealthy families; We never assumed that with the solid influences and examples we were instilling in our son, that these outside values would rub off and have such a profound effect on him. Looking back however, it was good that we provided a solid platform for him to bounce his exaggerated ideas off of, instead of us just bouncing him.

Guideline Number Sixteen: Anchor your child with solid values because when they enter the world these principles will be tested.

As I said earlier Joseph had this incredible champagne appetite, apparently not realizing that we were living on a strict beer budget! I'm not suggesting that we were poverty stricken by any stretch, but we were clearly a working class family, attempting to save as much as possible in order to accumulate some portion of that fleeting American dream. It was during one of our Saturday afternoon drives through the Capital Hill area of Seattle, following one of his little league baseball games at Montlake Community Center, that his adjustment to our reality began to take shape.............

"Dad, I need some Air Nikes! When can we go shopping?"
"Joe, we just bought you some baseball cleats and some
new dress shoes. That set us back one hundred-thirty dollars.

The Power Shift

Besides, what happened to the tennis shoes we bought you just two months ago?"

Then I gave him that old classic standby statement that verified the fact that I had truly become a parent. "What do you think I'm made of MONEY?" At first he stared, then glared at me and said, "First of all, pops, those shoes are outdated. The new version of Nikes are already being sold downtown. Besides, those other shoes ripped last Friday. They were cheap anyway! Man! Why does everything around here always come down to money anyway?" he angrily inquired.

During the lengthy silence that followed I began to count to ten, in the hope of saying the correct thing while being mad as hell at my son's new found cavalier attitude and total disregard for our hard earned money. I read somewhere you were suppose to count to ten instead of clobbering your child. Lucky for him I read it.

My count had reached forty when I responded with, "Ripped! Boy you're just too damn hard on shoes. For your information, the reason why most things come down to finances is that money is tight with private school and all your other expenses. The truth is Joe, sometimes we have to pinch pennies in order for you guys to get everything you really need."

I felt terrible saying that to him because as parents we generally want to be able to provide everything for our children, even though some things are not reasonable. Of course, Joseph was not buying my reasoning. "What I really NEED dad are some Air Nikes! Man, I wish we were rich. That way I could have anything I wanted." Hmm. That sounded familiar. "Joseph, even if we were rich, you still wouldn't get just anything you wanted. If we did that you wouldn't develop an appreciation for anything!"

Again sounding somewhat old and predictable, as well as

The Teacher In Every Parent

frustrated by now. I watched him roll his eyes in disgust at me after listening to my profound reasoning about money.

After some quiet time we drove by a fruit stand called the Rising Sun. We occasionally frequented it after his games. Joseph said, "You guys are too cheap for me! I need my own money so I can do what ever I want with it." After some pondering he asked, "You think they would hire me at Rising Sun?" Feeling that my son needed a dose of humility or reality or something, I agreed that we should find out. I turned the car around, drove to Rising Sun and instructed him to go in and request an application for employment. I purchased some peaches while I waited. That same day we filled the application out and rehearsed what would be said in the event of an interview. To my surprise, upon returning the application, Joseph was hired on the spot! He was excited and I was somewhat pleased for him. Puzzled, but pleased.

Instead of going home I turned around and headed due north to the mall. As a reward for getting hired, I bought him some expensive Air Nike Flights. The price ... A staggering one hundred-eight dollars. I told him with all the conviction I could muster that I would never purchase another pair of shoes for that price again in life! He was so happy however that he was quite amiable in his response. Small consolation for my check book, however.

For the next two weeks, my son diligently went to work after his baseball practices and stayed at his grandma Ruth's until he was picked up by one of us in the evening. Everything went as planned until that magical time arrived. PAYDAY! The boy's two week salary was one hundred-sixty nine dollars and forty-seven cents. (I should have subtracted my hundred-eight dollars! Of course, I didn't.) You would have thought it was a millions bucks. He was beaming from ear to ear, proud of his accomplishment

The Power Shift

and his monetary reward. As he pranced around the house showing off his first check to anybody who was not sick of viewing it, his mother asked him what he planned to do with it. He said proudly, "Well, spend it, of course!" She promptly took it. The boy went hysterical! He began screaming, crying, and pleading his case to his sympathetic grandparents. His mother said, "Joseph let me make a copy of it and then we can frame it for you. " He looked at her and painfully asked, "What about the original check mom? When can I cash my money?" "I'll add it to your savings account, honey," she said.

I observed the events unfolding and tried to maintain my composure, knowing he'd be coming in my direction shortly. Confrontation time: "Dad, are you going to let her get away this? You said that a man has to pay his own way in the world. You said that you have to pay the cost to be the boss. You said I had a champagne appetite. I'm trying to help you guys out. I'm feeding my appetite! You said that if I showed initiative and earned my own money, I could spend it as I pleased. You're not being hypocritical, are you?" Ten years old. Um. "I know what I said Joe! I don't need to be reminded." What could I say? The kid had me. I was left with few options because he had fulfilled every part of his obligation. "Sonja, let's go for a walk around the block and discuss the situation." We were normally together on such matters. She knew that I would stand behind any decision she made whether I agreed with it or not. My dilemma was I could see my experiment of teaching him independence and personal responsibility going right down the proverbial drain.

We went around the block and for one of the few times ever, I pulled rank on her. Joe got his one hundred sixty-two and forty seven cents to do with as he wished. The boy has been making and spending money ever since! His mother had the right idea. I should have listened her reasoning. I take full responsibility for the fact he has never developed any real saving habits. Although relatively speaking, he was much better than most of his peer group. His sister on the other hand is a miser! She had several thousand dollars saved by the time she graduated high school.

There was a shift in the power base for us as parents that summer. If you're smart and wise, you'll shift with it.

Guideline Number Seventeen: There's a time to relinquish a portion of the power. Recognize and do it gladly. Share that power with your young person.

From the ages of ten to sixteen (fourteen to sixteen in particular) the role of power and your interaction with it will change dramatically. In families our power base will decrease. Because of this shift we become less of the primary conduit of authority in the lives of our young people. During this time they start spending more hours outside of the home, interacting with people whose views may not be shared by the family. That is why it's especially important that the original power base have a solid platform. It's perhaps the only way to keep them grounded to the original principles as they enter this crazy, opinionated world of ours.

If our teaching has been consistent and the children have been learning exactly what our expectations are for them, great things can be asked of them. Our increasing demands are fine as long as we are supportive of them in every way. These expectations, along with their personal commitment, will later be the driving force in keeping them on right track.

Guideline Number Eighteen: Adults who sacrifice time and effort should expect to realize their child's total potential.

The Power Shift

There have been several studies done recently in an attempt to determine whether children of passive or authoritarian parenting fair better in the long run. Most of the studies seem to indicate that children of authoritarian parents seem to perform better than most children of passive parents.

According to Lawrence Greene's, <u>Smarter</u> <u>Children</u>, most kids of authoritarian parents tend to develop more self discipline and better decision making skills. Passive parenting allows children to explore their world with few checks and balances. This can sometimes be dangerous for a young person not prepared to process information. We all know that at some point children need to develop power over themselves, however, they need to be shown how to do so. Guidelines, limits, discipline and structure are key components in the development of strong positive children—creating what I like to call 'personal power.'

In the beginning, authoritative parents allow their children little power. In this theory, power, like money is earned by the child through progressive achievement. The parents are responsible for every action of that child and will devise rewards and consequences. As they increase in age, their power, responsibility and expectations should increase as well. This is how we attempted to parent. Many parents don't believe in this parenting style. They feel that children, regardless of their chronological age, should freely explore their world. These parents believe that the child will be far more equipped if they are exposed to everything. The earlier the better. This could work out in the end but there no evidence to back it up.

Have you ever watched a western and seen a run-away stagecoach with no driver and spooked horses? Those four legged animals will generally run wild until they're reeled in by the hero. This does not happen in real life unfortunately with a runaway child.

The Teacher In Every Parent

It is my opinion that anything given freely will be abused! Power is no exception. Remember that old saying, 'Power corrupts, and absolute power corrupts, absolutely. Many times something terrible has to happen before the young person realizes their mistake. Sometimes it's an unwanted pregnancy or failing grades in school. At times it's drug addiction or even gang involvement. Unfortunately sometimes death is the end result. These are just few of the consequences of such a run away stagecoach. We pulled on the reins and educated our children early on. We taught them how to think independently and expected a great deal from them. I'm not sure this will work for every parent, but I do know this direction worked for us. It was done with love, respect and purpose. If your children remind you of ours, try it and see if it works for you.

NINE

GUILT FREE PARENTING

*"It's not hard to make decisions
when you know what your values are."*

Dr. Anna Nicole Law

Autumn 1988

We decided to remove Joseph and Jawanna from the public school system in 1987 and enroll them in a private African American Parochial School in Central Seattle. We did this for a variety of reasons. Initially we were able to deflect the undercurrent of growing mediocrity in the Seattle public education system through our total parental commitment and involvement. We continued to scrutinize and encourage teachers, counselors and administrators. We remained active in the PTA and other school related activities in an attempt to better the school conditions for teachers, as well as for our children. In the end however, we decided to change schools in an attempt to buy our children a higher quality of education.

We also needed to remove them from the new wave of drugs and crime that had begun to infect the inner city of Seattle and it's schools. We had always planned to move them eventually but wanted them to get a taste of public school first. I thought children who went to private school initially, didn't handle the freedom of a public school environment well at all. Some kids just went wild!

Our decision was expedited by the attempted molestation of our daughter. This assault was further exasperated by the fact that the crisis was handled poorly by the principal of the school and the Seattle school district. They attempted to sweep the incident under the rug and avoid a public scandal. Jawanna was trapped and accosted in a restroom between class periods by two young assailants. Had it not been for her screams and a student wandering in, I believe she would have been sexually assaulted.

I was finally contacted at work three hours after the incident! I responded quickly but in my haste to comfort my daughter, I didn't think to contact Sonja. My reasoning stemmed partly from knowing in the past how she normally responded under certain critical circumstances. Not wanting her to worry about anything until I had the situation handled, I went to deal with it without her. I should have known better however. I was attempting to shoulder the responsibility. I blew it by not calling my wife first. Instead, I arrived alone trying to act like an unworried big shot. Unfortunately for me, Sonja never forgave me for that poor decision made in the fall of 1987.

In the end, the principal of the school was removed and admonished. The offenders involved were placed on two year probation for their part. That was all the reason we needed to bale out the public school system ahead of schedule. Without hesitation, off to a private school our children went.

Guideline Number Nineteen: Always consult your spouse or helpmate on everything. Who do you think you are anyway, the boss?

In spite of what many people outside the Pacific Northwest thought about Seattle, statistically, it had become the twelfth largest city in violent crimes in the United States. Three years prior, this once ugly, rain soaked fishing and lumbering town had been voted by many national magazines as the "most livable city"

Guilt Free Parenting

in the United States. Although Seattle had grown into a beautiful city, many negative changes had begun to happen. When people thought about drugs and the crimes that followed, cities like New York, the District of Columbia, Chicago, Los Angeles, Detroit, and New Orleans immediately came to mind. However, in the good old, sleepy, safe haven of the Pacific Northwest, Seattle's youth violence and gang activity was at an all time high. Much of this crime was being perpetrated by non-white children against non-white children.

Gang activity had been receiving much publicity in the Los Angeles area in the early 80's, and politicians who were seeking re-election, promised to stomp out crime in LA. This prompted many gang members to disperse and relocate to different parts of the country. A percentage ventured into Northern California, Portland, Oregon, Tacoma, and finally Seattle, Washington. Gang signs and gang paraphernalia were being flashed on a regular basis by rival groups that had infiltrated our neighborhoods attempting to recruit additional members and stake out new territories. A week before we enrolled our children in their new school, a twelve year old girl was shot in the face by a gang member for flashing a rival gang sign while traveling with her mother. It was later discovered that the child had recently learned the sign in school and was not even aware of its significance. The weekend before, a mother honked her horn in an attempt to get by a vehicle that was blocking traffic. Three young men turned and fired into her vehicle, killing the woman's two-year-old daughter.

Young boys in the Seattle area were routinely being robbed at gun point of their gold jewelry, starter jackets and high priced sneakers. Being inexperienced parents at the time, we had fallen victim to some of the peer influences ourselves, and had rewarded our children for a job well done by purchasing some sports jackets for them. An incident on Seattle's Metro transit where Joseph was nearly relieved of both his Air Nike shoes and his Notre Dame jacket motivated us to take his garments from him. He was allowed to wear them only while accompanied by one of us. He didn't like or understand what we did but we didn't care because we knew what was happening to others kids could easily happened to him. We had to do what was best for them, whether they liked it or not.

In our search for a good private school, we discovered that the best schools were not culturally diverse, in curriculum or enrollment. After much searching we finally found St. Theresa School which was located in the central area of Seattle, in the Madrona district.

As a teenager, I had grown up in that area and knew it well. We met with the head master, Wayne Melonson. I didn't know him personally, although, I knew most of his younger brothers who were around my age. The were a very large, gregarious Catholic family that excelled both academically and athletically. Our paths had crossed many times through the years. I liked and admired them.

As a youth, I desired to attend the St. Theresa school. Financially however, it was impossible, so I resigned myself to attending public school and make the most of it. From the beginning we were impressed with the school and thought it would be a great one for our children. They were enrolled in January 1987, and of course, fought us tooth and nail, putting up a barrage of verbal debates in our family meetings. They were leaving behind their friends, and the fear of the unknown had taken hold of them.

Guideline Number Twenty: Make the unpopular decisions quickly and decisively.

Guilt Free Parenting

With our usual spirit and vigor, Sonja and I dove head first into St. Theresa's School. There was a vacancy in the coaching area so I volunteered as boys basketball coach. We both got involved in the parent advisory board of the school. Sonja was fiercely protective of her children and we wanted to make sure they had every advantage. She also has been known to go off the deep end when they were not treated just right. We quickly discovered a couple of dramatic differences between public and private schools. Unlike the school system we left behind, this setting didn't welcome our impromptu visits or our suggestions during the board meetings.

Other parents who had children enrolled in the school from the first grade, were the ones who carried the most weight and influence. We were acknowledged by many parents as outsiders who should just pay their tuition, sell the mandatory amount of candy and keep quiet! In the past, we had relied on these visits of ours to keep the children involved and motivated. We grudgingly gave them up. We also discovered that parochial schools were run by a few power hungry type parents who weren't receptive to our style of parenting. Sonja told me about an older parent who had whispered some unwanted advice her way during a parents' meeting. "I had to put this lady in check tonight," she told me. "Oh yea, what happened?" I inquired. "They were asking for suggestions for new fundraising ideas and I offered one that had worked for us in the past. This snooty lady next to me said, 'Baby, you haven't been here long enough to offer any comments. It's best to just sit back and go along with the program for now, OK.' "Can you believe that! She must have really been trippin' trying to tell me what's best for my children. Pleeease!!" What she was beginning to realize was what I had already discovered. We were definitely outsiders in this political beltway. This didn't bother us though, because we had never been insiders in the first place. At this school we had to make appointments "one" week in advance to visit our children in class! I believe they thought we would be looking over their shoulders and critiquing, instead of assisting them.

This new attitude annoyed me because I found out that many of the teachers just didn't want to be caught looking ineffective at their jobs. We complied primarily because we were encouraged by the safety that was provided by the campus on a daily basis.

To further illustrate the difference this private school was from any public school we had seen, I once encountered a smug receptionist when I dropped by the school and checked in at the office for an impromptu visit with my children. "Do you have an appointment for today because I don't notice your name on my calendar, Mr. Smith?" "My name wouldn't be on any list miss." I said. "I just dropped in to check on my children—maybe have lunch, you know. I'll only be about twenty minutes or so." The receptionist looked at me strangely and said, "Put your name in my appointment book and I'll see you next week. It will be more convenient then."

"So are you implying that it's not a convenient time now?" I responded, with an engaging smile trying to encourage her to relax her guard. "Ah," she said. "You catch on quick..... Good day."

When my additional persuasion failed to yield the necessary response with the counselor, I pulled rank on her which enabled me to sit in on a portion of the class. I could see how unsettling my visit was on the teacher, although it added some needed reassurance for Joseph and Jawanna. From that time on however, our visits were strictly on an appointment basis.

Joseph and Jawanna were making some adjustments of their own. In an attempt to escape from some of the problems of the inner city, we moved to the north end of Seattle into a predominately Jewish neighborhood. Through this experience,

Guilt Free Parenting

most of their friends were caucasian although, Jawanna had what I used to term a "rainbow coalition" of friends. Joseph, on the other hand, had gone a giant step further by selecting only Caucasian friends to be in his world. This disturbed me a great deal. As far as I was concerned, exclusivity of any type meant something of value was not being included. Of course, St. Theresa school was approximately ninety-five percent African American. On the surface that appeared not to be a problem. However, while in public school, our children had got the label of being "whitified" by some of their peers. To my chagrin, our dilemma wasn't whether our children would be accepted by Caucasians children at St. Theresa, but whether they would be accepted by other African American children!

Overall however, we found St. Theresa to be a positive experience for them, as well as for ourselves. Although we never felt totally welcome or accepted as parents, the children generally had a pretty good time. They benefited greatly from the smaller class sizes, blended in and were accepted by the other children. They were also learning how to "hip hop" and "be down." (Both were invaluable ingredients in being accepted by your peer group.) I even guided the seventh grade Catholic Youth Organization basketball team to it's first winning season in fifteen years, losing in the semi-finals.

After a couple of years, we discovered the school to be just a step behind academically from the other private schools we had interviewed. We transferred them to St. Joseph on Capital Hill, knowing full well that we would be sacrificing some cultural diversity for a more overall challenging curriculum.

The children, like many kids didn't agree with many of our decisions regarding where they went to school or who we thought they should associate with. I'm proud of them however, for not rebelling against our long-term plans. They showed wisdom beyond their years and much confidence in us. I will always love and respect Joseph and Jawanna for that. In many ways they were a direct reflection of us. We were young parents attempting to provide the best for our children. We were relying strictly on faith and had very little working knowledge. (Especially in the beginning) Sonja and I really didn't know what was going on initially, but we rolled up our sleeves and dug in. Eventually we became above average parents. Our children didn't have a clue either, although many times they acted as though they did!

Guideline Number Twenty one: Set the pace for your child's life and normally they will emulate it.

The needs of a child demand much of our time and challenges us daily. This burden should be shared by both parents, if at all possible. Parental guilt can sometimes be an exaggerated manifestation of our own childhood experiences that we pass on to our children. For example, if we are afraid of the water, we generally stay away from it and request that our children do the same. Like most adults, I had my own hang-ups long before I became a parent. Those feelings were brought about by my own past experiences and definitely affected my parenting style. It will affect yours as well, and you should be aware of it. I still have a fear of snakes that was brought on by the fear and anxiety my mother had of the slithery things.

I discovered from conversations with my adult twins that moving traumatized them when they were younger. Of course, the children only moved three times while they were growing up. When I was growing up, we would sometimes move three times in one year! I vividly recall standing up in class and introducing myself to the class in an attempt to make new friends. Then I would work my way through that uncomfortable time of being

Guilt Free Parenting

accepted by peers, —just in time to move again. Since I relocated a lot, I naturally felt my children could handle the experience, after all, there are some benefits from relocating. I developed pen pals all over the world. (Obviously, this was before personal computers and electronic mail.) Mistakenly, I was raising them with my own experiences in mind. I could not have been more wrong.

However, one of a child's greatest pleasures early in life is to please their parents. Besides, there was very little that could be done. Through their conversations I learned that there was a negative consequence of my frequent relocating as a child. Generally, I have a nomadic mentally because of all of my constant travel as a child. Today, meeting people is a very easy task for me, however, I hold very few long term friendships. I'm always afraid that a separation might occur and normally keep a deliberate distance. Generation after generation, we have raised children with our own stored up anxieties, fears and expectations in mind. We only come to this realization later in life, after we go to counseling because of our own depressions, migraine headaches, marital difficulties or career problems that have manifested themselves through these feelings we acquired as children. My mother used to say, "The apple doesn't fall too far from the tree." Her translation: The combination of the two people involved in the union of a child, will generally determine what that child will be. Genetically, our children come fully equipped with most of our tendencies, mannerisms, behavior patterns and physical features.

A parent should not expect lesser achievements from their children than they were able to deliver when they were young however. Don't expect or sit still for straight D's from your child if you and your mate didn't make straight D's. If you were an excellent student with superior concentration, expect the same of your children. I agree with my mother. Of course, the child's

The Teacher In Every Parent

environment will effect them either way as well.

Today, I often hear parents say things like, "It's just a teenage thing that they're going through. He'll grow out of it." Or "She's just going through a phase. All children do it around this age." I believe that a parent receives EXACTLY what they expect to receive. Never expect your children to conduct themselves like other children! Taking that theme one step further, we used to tell our children to watch what the other young people around them were doing and purposely attempt to do something different. If there was an altercation and most of the children were running towards the disturbance, simply go the other way! It's not popular, just smarter. We never wanted our kids to be just like all the other children. It may sound arrogant, but, we wanted them to be a cut above the rest.

In retrospect, I believe they were, because we prepared and expected them to be!

An old mentor of mine once said to me, "Average is just the worst of the best and the best of the worst. You never want to fall into that category attempting anything." If you don't give them the extra support needed to succeed, expect mediocrity. Give them that additional help. (Extra tutoring, mandatory homework, question/answer time, extra weekly book reports, educational field trips, watching-observing time, etc,) A time that I enjoyed immensely was when Jawanna, Joseph and I would sit in the mall and just watch people—especially young people. Sonja didn't have the patience for such activities.

We used this time not to judge, but to evaluate verbal and physical communication. We studied body language and style of dress. We also observed many young people running in gangs, perpetrating as gangsters or pushing strollers. I would ask them their opinions about things that members of their peer group were doing. A great deal of knowledge was gained and shared by all of us during this time. This time also taught me to be more open minded about opinions that I didn't necessarily share. At times after lengthy discussions with our children we still had the responsibility of making the executive decisions. Not all of the decisions worked out either. When they occasionally didn't, I was always the first one to apologize to them. I never gave up the rank, however, because the job of parents— by example and with tough, sometimes unpopular decisions—is to lead, period!

Guideline Number Twenty-two: Make it clear that you don't have all the answers. Be quick to say, "I'm sorry."

TEN

SINGLE PARENTING

Where love exists, there is no labor; and if there be labor,
that labor is loved.

—Trevor Austin

July 1991

I found out first hand about the complexities of being a single parent when, after fourteen years of marriage I officially became one. Although my situation was somewhat unique in that after the separation and divorce, I saw my children practically everyday. They both had paper routes in their Mount Baker neighborhood, and when I got off work I would assist them, especially on Sundays. It was also strange in as much as neither of us wanted a divorce.

Even today, people who have known us for years are surprised when they discover that we are no longer married. Some people just look as though they fit and are suppose to be together. We were like that, I imagine. However, there were mounting pressures involved that eventually took its toll on both of us. We had both spent so much time concentrating on parenting that we forgot to take inventory of the needs of our marriage.

In the past while the children were growing up, we had always planned one weekend a month that was devoted completely to us. Sometimes we would go to Canada or Ocean Shores for the weekend. Occasionally, we would let the children spend the night with friends or relatives, while we would go to a nice restaurant, movie or a play.

For a many years this kept our marriage alive and fresh, which can be a difficult proposition when you have children who were into as many extracurricular activities as our kids were. As parents we tried to be a major player in every aspect of their lives. In my opinion, however, what lead to the ultimate demise of our marriage was the fact that, we simply weren't ready for the daily grind of being struggling young parents. I must say though, Sonja and I gave our marriage a hell of a try. We fought hard to make it work and the experience for all was well worth it. We realized success beyond our wildest expectations. The children benefited immensely! In the end however the pressure took it's toll.

My advice, based on years of experience is: If at all possible WAIT!!! Allow yourself time to grow and mature emotionally. If you are already a young parent, try to pull it all together. Realize that I'm not talking about getting married for the sake of the children. However, I do believe that our kids deserve better! If nothing else, you'll give your children a fighting chance. I know the development of our children was definitely worth the time I invested.

Guideline Number Twenty three: You owe your marriage or relationship as much attention as you do your children.

There were also growing concerns involved in my attempt to maintain a stable financial platform in corporate America. Since leaving college, I had been involved in everything from real estate sales to financial services, both as an agent and a broker. There were also several occupations in between in my quest to find my place in the corporate world. As ambitious as I was, things just

The Teacher In Every Parent

weren't happening fast enough for me. I was making a decent living, but I just was not experiencing success.

Many of you already know that there's far more to success than dollars and cents. I was searching for something I could find passion in.

However, the opportunities to create that fire needed to fuel my career seemed few and far between. Without attempting to make excuses for my circumstances, the bottom line was that corporate America and I were not getting along. Unfortunately, it was all I knew how to do.

I recently was explaining to a friend that when I was a young man, I read a book by John T. Molloy entitled <u>Dress</u> <u>for</u> <u>Success</u> from cover to cover, twice. In this book, everything was discussed from personal grooming, which included how to tie a Windsor knot, to the type of suit that was acceptable for normal business practice. It also spoke about how to conduct ones' self in a job interview. I became an expert in this topic because I needed to look the part in order to fit in and be successful. I was so impressed by what I had read that I incorporated practically every component of that book into my personal arsenal. If I was not going to be a success in Corporate America, I definitely was going to look like one!

This was to be part of my passionate attempt to make a splash in corporate America. I also studied, read and worked long grueling hours to become more proficient; however, I just wasn't making it.

After thirteen struggling years however, I discovered the reason for this dilemma. I was a rebel in a structure where rebels were rarely tolerated. By being a rebel, I mean I was an independent thinker in a environment where group thinking was the norm. Sort of an "out of the box" thinker on many topics. However, I was too young and ignorant to know that when department heads asked for my opinion or suggestion, they really didn't want either! I was and continue to be an original thinker who thought he was supposed to express himself when he had discovered a better way.

That's what the book had said. (I was really an entrepreneur at heart).

In every position that I was ever employed, I never resigned or was relieved because of my performance—something I'm extremely proud of. On occasion I was asked not to return though! Fired......Imagine that!! Something to do with being a disruptive flow—going against the corporate grain. I just wanted to get things done in a timely fashion, what's wrong with that? There's something about waiting until the twenty-third hour to get a project done that still pisses me off. I made another miscalculation as well. I believed that job performance was the prime employment criteria. Couldn't have been further from the truth. I discovered other criteria's such as: CYA, Cover your ass. BSC, Back Stabbing Colleagues. TTR-HTH, Throw The Rock, Hide The Hand!

Sonja began blaming my stubbornness as the problem. We began to argue about everything. In the end, we mutually felt that we loved, but no longer liked each other's style. At any rate, I suddenly began to experience the down side of family life after becoming a single, secondary parent. Of course, even after becoming divorced, we continued to celebrate birthdays and other special occasions together. We also continued our traditional family meetings. After all, we were still a family.

Guideline Number Twenty four: Personal
circumstances are no excuse for not being the best parent you can possibly be.

The Teacher In Every Parent

As long as God was the centerpiece of our universe, our family unit purred like a freshly tuned engine. We were thankful for everything in life; large or small. Our peaks were as high as the sky and our valleys were but small trenches. We prayed every morning as a family before the start of our day and at conclusion of the day, gave thanks for the blessings received. We were living a charmed life and the family was being showered with blessings.

As a man, living his life the world, I began to have my faith tested: A test by God that I failed. As my personal life began to unravel, (I suffered a mid life crisis at thirty-two!) I turned my back on God. I blamed him for my circumstances and wondered aloud, "How could He allow this to happen to me?" Why would he forsake His people; me a child of God. With all the terrible things that were happening in the world, I even briefly questioned His existence. The more I struggled with my dilemma, the further away from God I got.

I had forgotten where all my blessings had come from. I had forgotten that God is not only a miracle worker, but a caretaker as well. My situation could have been worse if not for him. I had forgotten that God works in mysterious ways as well. I had forgotten that God worked through people. I had forgotten to read my bible to renew my faith. I had forgotten how far God had taken my family, and how he had watched over our children. I had forgotten a great many things. I isolated myself in order to figure out what my next move would be. The obvious move should have been to drop to my knees and give thanks for the all blessings he had bestowed upon me. I'm renewed today and continue to be blessed by God's presence in my life. However, walking away from God actually cost me my marriage. That is something that can never be recovered. The best I can do is to advise others who are willing to listen.

Coming from primarily, a single parent environment, I

Single Parenting

certainly knew that this was not a new phenomenon in this country. From the age of seven until my mother remarried at the age thirteen, I was the child of a single parent. According to 1995 census bureau reports, four in ten European American households listed a single parent as the sole provider. In African American, Latino, and Native American households the ratio is as high as six in ten. Asian Americans comprise the smallest percentage at two in ten of these households.

In the United States it's still considered quite normal to have and maintain traditional-looking families. Unlike many societies where shared responsibilities of parenting are considered quite normal, single parenting in America is still viewed as a fragmented, dysfunctional component of child rearing. It shouldn't be thought of in this manner because, it normally takes many people to successfully raise a child. In most countries brothers, sisters, uncles, aunts, grandfathers or grandmothers all actively participate in raising children.

In America, the stigmatizing brought on by being the child of a single parent often times has an adverse affect on our children. A children of single parents must adjust to life with only one biological parent in the home. They also change residences, schools, and friends more frequently than kids of two-parent households. This makes growing up much tougher than it should be! That was one of the driving factors in my attempting to keep our parent-child relationship as normal as possible, in spite of the divorce. There was one event I recall, when having no father had a momentary stigmatizing effect on me. It happened while I was a member of the Cub Scouts of America. Our troop leader announced their annual Father and Son Weekend. I had spoken to my Uncle Charles about accompanying me to the outing. He agreed, however he had to work late and was unable to attend the event. My best friend's father was kind enough to take me along with them, however, I didn't feel that I really belonged because everyone had somebody of their very own except for me. That was the longest weekend of my life. I quit the scouts shortly afterward.

Single parents are described as simply anyone with some form of legal custody of their children and no live-in partner. The parent may have been divorced, widowed, or never married. I need to say that I have always maintained the utmost respect and admiration for single parents, even before I became one.

Single mothers receive special kudos here. Although, I must also say that single fathers are an ever increasing component in the single parenting equation. Many men are doing a very credible job. One of my best friends, Larry Evans, is a single father with sole custody and is doing a fantastic job with his son. I also have a friend who I believe is under the mistaken impression that in every husband-wife relationship, the man generally makes six-figure salaries! She also feels women should stay home and tend to needs of the family and not be involved in the work place at all. In this scenario, the housewife would dutifully escort her children to their youth activities and perhaps do some volunteer work in the community to round out her schedule.

She was born in the early 50s and therefore was a product of the 1950's and 60's, influence. An era incidentally that I hold dear to my heart because it represented a time where things were somewhat slower, simpler and less intrusive. A time where mother would stay home and bake bread instead going to the bakery. A time where staying home to raise the children was more respected than it is today. A time when you could buy a home for five thousand dollars and one income was sufficient to support a family. A TIME UNFORTUNATELY GONE BY.

As a single working mother with two children to support, Ramona Bigham's frustration was a simple one to evaluate. She had grown up in a very special traditional home, and as is normally the case, acquired traditional values.

In the last twenty years many of those family values have been violently shaken and eroded. They have been replaced with new, self serving values. As a result, the values she finds herself facing today grossly conflict with her inherent ones.

Being single, there is also precious little time to organize any after school or summer programs for her children. She told me that she doesn't understand why so many recreational programs cater the majority of their youth activities for mid-day and early afternoon time schedules. There is barely enough time for her to attend the extra curricular activities her children participate in. She feels these programs are discriminatory. While I agreed that many of these programs are scheduled at inconvenient times, I tried to assure her that there was no overall conspiracy involved. Most community centers have programs throughout the day and pay special attention to the needs of a particular neighborhood. She wasn't buying any of this. She believes it to be a set up that favored two-parent households. Ignoring this, my suggestion to her was that since she loved organizations (this woman was a member of several) she join the neighborhood recreation center in order to influence their scheduling. More importantly there would an opportunity to meet other parents who shared her concern. She has slowly accepted that with the increases in mortgages, vacation homes, car notes, braces, and other expenses generally associated with living a decent life, it normally takes a two parent income to make a home function fully, from a financial standpoint anyway. As a single parent this financial hardship can be a difficult one to endure.

It is an equally difficult problem for men as well. Across the United States, approximately 1.3 million men are single parents. This number has doubled over the last ten years. Although that is

The Teacher In Every Parent

far less than the seven million mothers who are going at it alone in this country. Men's attitudes are beginning to change as well. "You have to pitch in man. Otherwise, you don't stand a chance. Things become overwhelming," said Ed Steward, a business executive whose wife works as an engineer. Even though their jobs keep them hopping, many men have decided that developing relationships with their children far outweighs the total career objectives. In most law firms and the medical profession, cutting back hours to tend the needs of the family is actually frowned upon. Billing hours and being on call twenty four hours a day is viewed as far more important.

Of course, this is slowly changing with men's newfound need for full recognition in the total child rearing process. Men are beginning to see the opportunities of total family involvement. Housework may not be easy or fun, however, being with their children is. For example, Roger Dunn says he goes to bed around nine o'clock p.m. and usually wakes about four o'clock a.m. The main reason for this ritual is his two children. Katherine and Ross, are three years and one year. "If I cut corners (at work), I couldn't live with it. So what I do is get less sleep," he said. This shift is especially evident in families where the financial responsibilities are shared by both parents. After all, I think about life's priorities what could possibly be of more importance than raising and providing for a child?

However, just when men are trying to be active fathers, competitive pressures at most work places are increasing. I believe that parents, employers and the public sector need to work together on practical solutions. If we lose our children while attempting to maintain careers, society will be the big loser in the end.

There are several components of single parenting. There are many parents who remain single by choice. Some single females I

Single Parenting

spoke with even admitted a desire for children, but not a mate! In 1995 alone, there were over one million teen pregnancies in the United States. Fifty percent of these pregnancies were carried to full term.

A reverse stigma is occurring today because of the proliferation of unwed parents. The consequence is that single parenting is now thought to be, in many circles, more normal and acceptable than having two parents! Twenty five years of this new phenomenon has created an undercurrent of rebellion among children of traditional family homes. Obviously some young people have surrendered to the peer pressure. Why some women have decided that single parenting is the answer is not totally clear to me. However, some cite individual control as a primary factor. From one standpoint some single parents I interviewed said that although they experience some personal hardships, they found it beneficial not having to consult or argue with another adult figure as far as decision making was concerned.

The majority these parents were strong-willed people who wanted total control of their household. They also felt they already had a complete handle on their family situations. Some were somewhat inflexible people who discovered that having, an opinionated mate around might, at some point, put them at a disadvantage.

Although most were adamant about their commitment to the single life, it's clear that these feelings will not always be the case. Statistically, it has also been proven that it is more difficult for an single parent to find a mate, something that most will desire at some point. In any event, I'm not sure these parents were thinking about the children when they made this assessment. I'm of the opinion that in this scenario, both parent and child will forever be at somewhat of a disadvantage.

Hollywood has contributed enormously to this new parenting

The Teacher In Every Parent

attitude as well. Influential actresses such as Margot Kitter, Jessica Lange, Cher and Whoopi Goldberg to name a few have been raising children in this manner for over a decade and a half. Whereas these celebrities still suffer many of same disadvantages of not having a male role model on the scene, financially speaking, they have a distinct advantage-something the average single parent in America can't say they have.

Another problem is the negative affect this lifestyle choice is having on our young people. It has become popular and trendy in our society to become a teenager with a child. I have two questions regarding this subject.

1) When did it become hip to push around strollers and go on public assistance?
2) Who is going to parent these children?

Many of these teenage parents either attempt to go back school, go directly to work in some minimum wage job or opt to go on public assistance. Given this rough beginning to parenting, its no wonder that many children have such a difficult time. As most of us know, parenting a child when you have some skills can be tough. Imagine the hurdle that both the child and parent have to deal with if those parenting skills are lacking. Unfortunately I'm hearing more about infant abuse, neglect, and disposal than I ever have in the past.

Once while at a bus stop, I observed five teenage girls between the ages of thirteen and fifteen. They were discussing pregnancy while comparing the sizes of their growing stomachs. They were boasting about who was going to be the first to deliver! Four of the five girls were visibly pregnant. The fifth young lady, who was not yet with child, looked somewhat envious. The others were putting her down because she hadn't gotten pregnant yet!

Single Parenting

My mind was momentarily blown away.

Women who suffer a divorce or are widowed unfortunately are many times being categorized along side women who have decided to have children out of wedlock. This is quite an unfair grouping.

We attended school with our children for the first time in 1980 and were shocked to discover how this stigma had attached itself to the children of dual parent households. When we entered our children in John Muir Elementary school, I was surprised by the number of single mothers who were roaming the halls with their children. While the halls were buzzing with activity, I could count the number of fathers in the building on one hand. As we entered the classroom many of the other children stared as if they had seen a ghost. Finally a little boy blurted, "Ooh! Joe and Jawanna have a mom and a dad!" It suddenly dawned on me that many of these children were growing up with no male role model in the home. To my surprise and dismay the traditional two parent household had been reduced to an oddity by the mid 1980s and many kids from those households felt somewhat left out in the cold.

Typically when a divorce or separation occurs, the man usually has far more flexibility in determining his immediate future than does the woman. Not being the primary parent in most cases means he generally has weekend and summer visitation rights where most of the fun activities occur. He is generally viewed in the eyes of the children as the "good parent" of the two and therefore has a much easier time with the children. He often-times has the option of whether to attend the children's school functions, and since he's not the primary parent, is rarely called when any trouble at school occurs. Then there is the long dist-tant parent. The type of guy that either runs away or makes life so unbearable that the spouse has to leave. I like to call this person the "totally out of touch" parent because he does

The Teacher In Every Parent

virtually no parenting whatsoever, leaving the entire burden of raising the child squarely on the shoulders of the mother and whatever support she can find. This parent's sole responsibility has been reduced to paying court ordered-child support. While most men are perfectly willing to assume their financial obligation, there are some who dodge even that duty.

Recently, there was an business executive who was arrested in Minnesota for back child support payments of $200,000! Many men pay their child support obligations regularly but this is nothing special. We are supposed to. However, this is only part of our parental duty. Most paying parents feel their responsibility ends once the finances are handled. While I am not attempting to rip men at this time, I am trying to point out the gross inadequacies that still exists today. There are, of course, many men who are single parents and are doing a good job of assisting in the raising of their children.

At times men suffer the same injustices that woman face. However, the fact is that men usually have the resources to recover quicker emotionally, financially, and psychologically from a divorce or separation than a women does. Especially a woman who is the primary caregiver.

Today's mothers are having to shoulder much of the burden of our children's day to day life, and sometimes receive very little appreciation from their own children in return. Usually the parent who tells the child when to go to bed, whether they can spend the night at a friends or to clean up their room, is viewed as the "mean parent." Women are unfortunately left with the sole responsibility of being this primary care giver and provider in most cases.

Recently, men's groups have surfaced to address equal rights and more equity in child support payments. They are also concerned about visitation rights for the secondary parent. They want to eliminate the use of children as the occasional bartering

Single Parenting

chips or as leverage to secure extra financial benefits. These support groups are a welcome and necessary part of our society today, because many women are as financially mobile as some men are.

As shocking as it may seem, women at times even neglect their parental duties. In visiting one of these groups, I had a conversation with a divorced man who told me how his former wife would insist that he pay additional (under the table) dollars or she would cancel his bi-monthly visitations with his daughter. I asked if he had sought counsel to rectify his problem. He told me that when he took his complaint to family court, he was told he had no recourse because he could not prove anything.

Although these situations do occur, the majority of women are loving, nurturing, providers who are usually attempting to make the best of a difficult situation. I'm aware of the many trials and tribulations my mother endured in attempting to keep five active boys on the straight and narrow path of life. Single parenting was generally a tough and isolating experience for her. She spent many lonely days and nights comforting us when she could have been doing other things with her time. When she was feeling exceptionally down, she would put Al Green or Marvin Gaye on the record player and rearrange her house. I believe that rearranging her home helped her maintain her focus in a sometimes scrambled life. Our place rearranged so often that at times, I did not know whose house I had entered. Sometimes when I arrived home from school, we would pretend we were in a ballroom and dance well into the evening. She was a good dancer. She taught me how to slow dance; I taught her to Waltz, and Tango. I enjoyed spending time with her because obviously I loved her. I also knew she was sacrificing a great deal for us. However, I secretly wondered why she didn't go out sometimes and have a good time. She later told me that she had to sacrifice for her children because it was her "number one responsibility." Besides, she said that overall, she was having a good time hanging out with us. When I recall her saying that, I always get goose bumps. Like many mothers, our mom was such a superior parent. When we got our summer jobs, we would generally support the household in anyway we could to help out. One of us might pay a utility bill, purchase a bag of groceries or just put some gas in the car. Taking her out to dinner was something my brothers and I always enjoyed doing as well. She never seemed to run out energy or ideas to make sure that the correct type of male influence was around us either. In my opinion, she was the original superwoman.

My mother used to say, "I had to be the mom and the dad for you guys." The times that she couldn't, she supplied many male role models around us on a daily basis until she remarried. My mother knew policemen, social workers, coaches, doctors and garbage men. Because she was fine, they were quite willing to come around! She knew how to strategically position them in our lives on some level depending on the circumstances, and they would give us that male guidance.

Guideline Number Twenty five: If you are not capable of supplying it, surround yourself with people who can.

Being the product of a single household had little outward negative effect on me, because most of my friends had two parents in their home. Growing up, I enjoyed going over to my friend's house because he belonged to a traditional looking family. It seemed like a functional, working family to me. They had a classic looking 'Leave it to Beaver' household. He had the dad that I was missing so I believed he had it made. It was years later that he shared with me what his family was really like. He told me that his father was a surly, non-communicative man who didn't take part in their lives on any level. Obviously, I was looking at the outside image and not the core. I guess the grass always appears greener on the other side.

As terrible as it sounds, not all two parent households are everything they are cracked up to be. Many married mothers I interviewed told me they felt like single parents because their spouses did not take an active role in the child rearing process. Several divorced and single working mothers also told me about the amount of anxiety this caused them.

Sometimes the combination of a parent's high expectations and a child's mediocre achievements can increase these anxious and frustrating feelings as well. I have known some parents to become overprotective of their children in every respect while attempting shield them. For example, if their child is not achieving academically, parents sometimes can become antagonistic toward the teacher or school.

In 1994, I worked in the Seattle public school system as a teacher-mentor in a program called the Burger King Academy. Meaning no disrespect, this was just another program that was throwing money at a huge problem. This program had not analize the problem long enough to realized the sources dilemma, and as usual they didn't supply enough money in the right direction. Well that's another topic for another time. There I discovered that at times the parent, usually a stressed out mother, would lash out at me for being the messenger of their child's mediocre progress. I didn't take the criticism personally because I knew they were besieged parents who were feeling overwhelmed by their circumstances.

Men are a necessary component in the development of values in our young people. However, many are 'missing in action" and

The Teacher In Every Parent

need to return to duty. With the exception of the Asian communities, men of color have been historically and systematically a missing link in the parenting equation. Although the reasons are complicated, we need to stop making excuses for our situations, roll up our sleeves and begin setting a better example for our children to emulate. Generally, most men spend so little time with their young children, they hardly know them. Our children will approach the parent they feel will be there for them in their time of need. The consequences of a man not being there for his children are that they will normally seek out their mother for help, instead of him. They may reject their father's offer of assistance completely. The scariest thought is if they look to their peer group (the street) for their support and guidance.

When watching a sporting event as a kid (usually a football game), I would frequently check out an athlete who, in his excitement, would turn to a camera and shout, "Hi Mom!" Unfortunately it was not "Hi Dad" or "Hi Uncle.' It was always, "Hi, mom." In viewing this behavior, this struck me as they were doing the right thing by acknowledging mothers. Most single mothers were the straw that stirred the family drink. They are the "bridge that crosses us over." Most mothers, in most families are as well.

ELEVEN

LETTING GO

My heart is heavy at the remembrance of all the miles that lie between us.
I can scarcely believe that you are so distant. We are parted and every parting
is a form of death, and every reunion is a type of heaven.

—Edwards

November 26, 1994
The twins 18th birthday

Once Joseph, who was about ten at the time, was being harassed by some older boys who were part of a street gang that had been recruiting new members in our area. This group of misguided hooligans called themselves the 'Black Gangster Disciples-BDG's for short. During this time, other gangs known as the Crips and Bloods were also popping up all over the place.

Several "wanna be" gang members were aligning themselves through the Seattle public schools as well. The fellas that had approached my son were the hard-core thug types who attempted to isolate and control kids through intimidation and violence. Their goal was to use these children to rob, deal drugs and recruit other members.

Knowing that my son could not yet handle himself in situations like these, I intervened on his behalf by going to where I was told the leader of this group could be found. To my surprise, I discovered that this hoodlum was several years older than I was! I caught up with this thirty-three year old criminal at a warehouse in Southwest Seattle that had been converted into a storage center

The Teacher In Every Parent

for stolen merchandise. Apparently this place also served as rendezvous point. He was having Joseph recruited to join something called 'his posse' and my only reason for being there was to inform him that this was never going to happen to my boy.

Our brief dialog went like this:
    "Look man, you can't mess with my son anymore."
    "What makes your son any different from anybody else?"
    "I have invested too much time and energy into him.
    I've got plans for his future."
    "So do I, my brotha. He joins my set or he's gon'
    have his ass stomped every day till he does."

After about fifteen seconds of silence, I said,
    "I ain't your brother. Don't touch him again."
    "Sounds like a threat fella. You prepared to back it up?
    Looks like you packin." I'm sho' as hell packin."
    What you wanna do?"

I was packing a gun all right. I'd actually stuffed my leather jacket with a rolled up towel. It must have looked like a gun. I knew it wasn't one because I don't care for the things. I finally said, "Yea, I'm packing' and..... I'm prepared to die for mine. Are you prepared to die?"

Guideline Number Twenty Seven: Sometimes
you must enter the lions den to save your child.

Afterwards, I remember thinking about that man and wondering why he wasn't trying to mentor these children in a positive way instead of the way he had chosen. Something tragic in his past, I guessed. Anyway, I never saw or heard from that

Letting Go

guy again, and fortunately my son was never approached again.

Scenarios like the one I just described happen every day in the inner cities, suburban and rural areas of America. I don't know why more parents don't stand up for their children. Nobody wants their child to fall prey to this sordid lifestyle, even if it's the only life the parents know. Although there is a great deal of fear created by these kinds of issues,.....letting go of our children is something we must do.

Shirley Gould, author of <u>How</u> <u>to</u> <u>Raise</u> <u>an</u> <u>Independent</u> <u>Child,</u> suggested that the more children we have, the easier it is for us parents to let go. That is not to imply that parents who have many kids don't care for their children as much as parents with fewer children. She merely suggests that with a large family, a parent must use time management more than ever while parenting. (My mother called this spreading the love around.) Many times older siblings assist with child rearing, making detaching slightly easier. Nevertheless, our final assignment as mothers and fathers is the discomforting task of releasing our young adult children and allowing them to launch themselves into this big, exciting, sometimes cruel world of ours. First, let us establish that this letting go process is an extremely difficult time for most of us. We were no exception, although I had been mentally preparing for it for a while. I really started to let go of them the year after our divorce when the children were fourteen. I went to their home, baseball glove in tow to grab Joe and play some catch. He and I had developed this special bonding ritual that had begun when he was only six years old and asked for a Rawlings baseball glove. Shortly afterward we attended his first Seattle Mariner baseball game.

Since that time, regardless of the weather, Joe and I played catch almost everyday of his life. That is probably where he fell in love with our American pastime. One this day, I brandished our mitts in full anticipation of his affirmative response. Today however he replied, "Not today dad. I'm going to play with a buddy of mine.

Maybe another time.....All right?" I never let him know how crushed I was by his response. Besides, he didn't mean any harm. He had just been expanding his own world. From then on, however, I began to mentally prepare for the inevitable. With Jawanna my withdrawal was slightly different. She had always considered herself "daddy's little girl," even though she clearly had outgrown that moniker. Even as a child, she sensed my lack of knowledge for her feminine side. I believe she appreciated the fact that I had grown up without sisters in my family. My detachment from her really began when she started kissing boys in the seventh grade. Again, I was really hurt because we had shared almost everything in the past. During that I time, I also learned that many young men attempt to isolate and control young ladies for their own benefit. Even so, it was still a difficult situation to handle. Of course, this process was eased by the fact that we had paid close attention to our parental responsibilities when they were young children. These preparations for letting go were also were made easier as our children were becoming more and more scarce in our lives on a daily basis.

Guideline Number Twenty Eight: As difficult as it may seem, let them go. They're like boomerangs; they will return!

Both of them had part time jobs, were active in sports and attended challenging schools. As part of preparing them for the next level, we encouraged the children to work and save. It began with lemonade stands and progressed to paper routes. While in private school, as part of raising funds candy had to be sold. We

Letting Go

never sold candy for them at work. (Well, I never did.) They were encouraged and shown how to solicit door to door. The hope was that the experience would increase their overall confidence and enable them to better meet challenges. Today they both sell themselves extremely well.

By the time they were graduating seniors, the children had made several thousands of dollars working at various jobs.

They had learned well. It was also quickly approaching the time when they would be almost completely on their own. As this time crept upon us, we begin to reflect on the job we had done as parents. How tightly you hold onto your child will generally be determined by how effective you believe you were as a parent. Most of the time we do an excellent job of teaching our children, however if there is any doubt it will show itself here.

As parents we care passionately for our children and will do anything to protect them and meet their needs. We are accustomed to loving, nurturing and involving ourselves in all aspects of their lives. Of course these same qualities also add to our difficulties when it comes to letting go of our sons and daughters.

Dr. Alvin F. Poussaint, Psychiatrist and Harvard University professor said in the Chicago Sun-Times, writing about so-called "good" parents: At the opposite end of neglectful parents, are the overly concerned and overly conscientious ones, who are so afraid of making a mistake that they stifle their children's growth....Some parents also want their children to be perfect, and therefore, they make subtle demands for exceptionally proper behavior." I wanted to be that rare parent who could teach his children to be independent, while letting them go when the time came because I believe that is when a young person truly develops. I discovered there are two components that make parents hold on so tightly. In James Dobson's book, entitled, *Parenting Isn't for Cowards,* he addresses overprotective parents. Control is factor number one. Consider this excerpt from his book:

"I am 21 years old and the eldest of three children. My parents are still overprotective. They won't let go. I have a career and a very stable job, but they won't allow me to move out on my own. They still try to discipline me using a belt and hold me to a 10:00 curfew. Even if it is a church activity, I must be home by 10:00. If it's impossible for me to be home by that time, I'm not allowed to attend or one of them must accompany me. I'm not allowed to date either. I have high Christian moral standards and they trust me, but they are just overprotective."

In this example, the young adult is partially at fault for allowing this to happen. There comes a time when young people are supposed to grow up and question authority. Not negatively, but critically. It is considered fairly abnormal when this is not done. When this questioning is done often enough, as parents, we usually reach an impasse with our young person moving out and beginning to adjust to life on his or her own. There usually are no hard feelings, only a slight adjustment. At some point we must come to grips with the realization that our children are now approaching adulthood and will begin to demand some extra space.

In the previous example, young adults who have yielded to this type of parental behavior, have and will continue to retard their own emotional growth. They also run the risk of setting back their adult relations with their parents for many years to come.

First Corinthians 13:11 says, *"When I was a child, I talked like a child, I thought like a child, I reasoned like a child. When I became a man, I put childish ways behind me."* Could there be anything more childish than a twenty-one year allowing her parents to spank her. The young person and the parents involved must realize there comes a natural time in their lives when it is considered normal

Letting Go

for them to expand their world. Parents who haven't developed a feel for knowing when it is time to loosen, and letting go of the reins, risk stunting the maturation process of their child-not to mention, increasing the burden to themselves. Parents who refuse to do this are flat out refusing to adjust to change!

Fear is factor number two. Once we were returning from playing tennis at our neighborhood park. Joseph and Jawanna were seven at the time, and as was his habit, Joe would walk several feet ahead of everyone else. On this Saturday afternoon he approached a four way stop one block from our home. A man driving a pickup truck stopped at the intersection and gestured to him to cross the street. When Joseph entered the intersection, the man slammed on the accelerator aiming his vehicle in my son's direction. His mother instinctively pulled him back by the collar, possibly saving his life that day. The man had deliberately attempted to run our son down! Being blinded by rage, I ran after the truck in an attempt to catch the guy. He stopped every twenty feet or so just to taunt me. Not once did I think to get his license plate.

It is almost impossible to explain the amount of fear that we had in the days that followed. Sonja wouldn't let the children out of her sight for anything. She was absorbed by fear and paranoia for the next week. She'd check on them several times a night during this period. Since it was summer, she even insisted on taking them to work with her. Near misses of any kind make us want to huddle our children around us in a protective mode. Since we couldn't do that twenty-four hours a day, we turned our fear into a positive situation. We developed a "family password" to ease our tension during the times when the children were not in our presence. They were instructed to run if they asked and did not hear the password. It did not matter if it was a relative or friend. "Valentine" was our secret word and with all the danger

The Teacher In Every Parent

that can come a child's way, I suggest every parent do the same thing!

As parents we are charged with the responsibility of nurturing, teaching, disciplining, correcting, and encouraging our children to mature and become the very best they can be. During this time, it is also extremely important that we understand the importance of their decisions. Although we will always be there for them as parents, we are also obligated to teach our children how to be responsible for themselves.

In a perfect world, we hope that our children never experience major risk or harm. Although this is a pipe dream, as far as I'm concerned, not properly preparing and letting them go can cause us far more harm than good. The idea of suggesting that your child do and think for themselves can be a frightening thought to many of us. I believe the main reason this thought scares us so is that there is no outward barometer to gauge the type of job we have done as parents. Did we complete the task of preparing our children or not?

Over the years, we have grown a accustomed to having our children in our lives on a daily basis. We also got used to our children soliciting our opinions on many topics when they were younger. Children need their parents on an exclusive basis—primarily in their first ten years of life. From then on, however, they require less parental time as they become more involved in school and peer group activities. This also can be a challenging time for us now that we have to deal with opinions from outside the home that may conflict with our values. This is OK because it is the beginning stage of letting go.

When I first moved away from home, my mother became paranoid over my departure. She called twice a day, everyday, for the first two weeks, straight, and would have come by if she could have. She would ask strange questions like, "Are you getting enough to eat? How late were you out last night? Are you going to bed on time?" Of course I wasn't eating correctly, nor was I going to bed at decent time. I was out most of the night! Later, she revealed that she was going through some unexplainable withdrawal anxieties. I assured her that everything was all right and apologized for adding to her concerns. I couldn't relate to her feelings completely until I had children of my own. Still I believe those feelings are experienced more acutely by women than men. Maybe it's a maternal thing. I'm not really sure. Generally, women are more sensitive to the concerns of our children than men are.

Once, I verbally admonished my son for behavior I deemed inappropriate for his age. He was six at the time. My problem was that I was expecting behavior that wasn't on par with his chronological age. An elderly woman observed me and meekly inquired, "Why did you embarrass your son in public like that?" As I was about to respond to her question the woman asked, "Do you normally talk to children like that?" As I was about to explain my position and his fault, she continued, "Your boy is going to be a adult longer than he's going to be a child. The earlier you learn to adjust your behavior to fit HIM, the quicker your child will respond to you. In that way he will never lose respect for you." I shook my head affirmatively as she walked away. I had realized my error. I was only twenty-five at the time, still trying to figure things out. I never saw that woman again and never forgot what she said.

I learned I had to alter my behavior and expectation to fit our children's appropriate chronological, emotional, and mental age. It also taught me that:

There is a time to hold their hands: In the beginning when they are looking to us for leadership and guidance.

The Teacher In Every Parent

There is a time to be an authoritarian: To correct them with firmness, love, and respect.

There is a time to be watchful and mindful: As they begin to put actions behind the thoughts we encouraged them to have. There are bound to be some parental differences.

There is a time to become a negotiator: As their world changes around them, they may acquire opinions that may differ from ours. When parental power begins to shift, we must learn to bargain, make deals and devise contracts.

Finally, there is a time to let go: Knowing that, as parents, we have done our best, we must also be aware that our children will trip and fall occasionally, while testing their wings. As we let our children go into world, we asked only one thing. Stay true to the our family motto. "Never do anything to embarrass the family. Always do something to enhance it" That rule was meant for the adults as well as our children.

TWELVE

ACTION PLAN
FOR CHANGE

I know of no more encouraging fact than the unquestionable
ability of a man to elevate his life by conscious endeavor.

—Henry David Thoreau

I am a self-taught tennis player who has been instructing youths and adults for some thirteen years. I discovered the game of tennis while watching Arthur Ashe win the United States Open as an amateur in 1968. Not seeing any other African Americans playing tennis at the time, led me to believe it was a white man's game. I was only eleven at the time. It was reintroduced to me when, again, the great Arthur Ashe defeated Jimmy Connors to win the Wimbledon Championships in 1975. This time I was going to do something about this game I growing to like so well. I went to Osborn & Ulland, a local sporting goods store and purchased an aluminum Wilson tennis racket. I immediately set out to the tennis court to find somebody to play with.

While enroute I ran into a couple of my running partners, and, while trying to conceal my excitement, showed off my brand new racket to them. They inspected it, looked at each other and one of them said, "You gone fag on us Joe? What's with the racket? Tennis is for sissies man. I know you ain't no punk." Since I played football, baseball and ran track with these guys, and not wanting to look bad in their eyes, I said the first natural thing that came to my mind. I lied!

"Naw, man this ain't my racket. I'm taking this thing over to my cousin's house. I think he signed up for some lessons or something."

Demetrius Pugh, the fastest and most athletic cat on our side of town responded, "Hmm, is your cousin a fag?" "No! he's not a fag!........ Look fellas, I gotta run, check ya later!" I immediately escorted my tennis racket and can of balls back to Osborn and Ulland and demanded my money back from the clerk. After a heated discussion, and while being reminded that I didn't have my receipt, I was granted a store credit for anything costing eighteen dollars, ninety-five cents. I promptly took it.

I didn't look at or think about tennis again until seven years later when Joseph and I were walking home from the park and witnessed two girls playing. "Dad, what's the name of that game?" "Tennis," I responded. "Do you know how to play it?" Sheepishly I said, "No, buddy, not yet." "Can we learn it together sometime? "he inquired. Absolutely.....When?.....Tomorrow? Great!"

While it was Arthur Ashe who was my introduction to the game of tennis, it was Joseph Jr. who was my inspiration to change an old attitude and initiate a new behavior. We began playing while reading a book entitled, Tennis for the Future by Vic Braden. In six months, I went from tennis hacker to 'A' player. I was instructing two years later. For his part, Joseph went on to become a ranked player in the juniors in the state of Washington for the next ten years. In fact by the age of nine, he was regularly pounding the ball against college level players. He was a tennis phenom. Regional coaches who traveled around looking for talented players, were constantly in touch with us attempting to recruit him. They began sending us all the demo rackets, balls, and supplying us with all the free court time we could handle. His development was so impressive that everyone who knew anything about the game, thought he was going to become a professional tennis player—Everyone but him. In spite of his ability, he wanted something else for his life. In spite of the fact that at the age of ten he struck the ball like a man, his desire was to just play the game socially, while concentrating on his team sports.

It didn't help that he defeated the number-one player in the state of Oregon in the 1988 Sea-Fair Tournament and was promptly called a skinny nigger. I've been called that derogatory name many times. It only served to inspire me, however, Joseph was deflated by it. He had grown weary of being the only African American child entered in the regional tournaments. I kept telling him that there would be other blacks kids coming. The only people of color who began to come were Asians. For whatever reason, most did not have a desire to associate with us.

Although I later started and coached a minority tennis team, my prediction of other African American kids coming never came true. That was all the incentive he needed to quit the game that I had fallen in love with. (Boy, I wished someone would have introduced me to the game of tennis at the age of six). Who knows.......

Guideline Number Twenty Eight: Make certain
that the child's dreams are not your own.

In all behavior modifications, creating a climate of change is a priority. This means giving any plan you decide to utilize top attention at all times during the day and mentally rehearsing the plan before acting on it. In dealing with your child from the beginning, discuss the issues initially. I used to say things like, "we've been making some mistakes lately. We're going to get started by doing something differently. I really need your help." Then I stated any problem clearly and allowed them to do the same from their perspective. I always attempted to be firm and respectful when implementing a new program with our children. I expected the same from them.

Many times our children don't understand the importance of their actions and the ramifications they may have. They also are not fully aware of what our reactions will be in response to their behavior. While every child is different, initially, expect your child to resist change. Did you not resist change initially? Don't we all? It's quite a normal course of action. It is the easiest course of action to take.

Human nature indicates that we all seem to follow the 'path of least resistance! Most of the time were are afraid to change an old, ineffective pattern in our life. That is why on average only three percent of us retire financially independent. Most of us get into a negative rut—be it physical, emotional, financial or mental—and we become unwilling or afraid to change. I plan to be in that three percent!

A friend who was trying desperately attempting to break a twenty-five year smoking habit once told me, "I keep trying, but this thing has a hold on me and won't let go." I would always ask him to describe the 'thing' that had such grip on him. He never could get specific about it. He knew he had a physical addiction caused by years of smoking and his body's dependence on nicotine. However, what I really wanted him to understand was his psychological addiction. For as smart as my friend was, he had forgotten the one basic concept: The mind controls the body. The basic science of mind over matter. The mental has always dictated to the physical. The problem arises when one allows the body to take over like my friend had. In that case, there would always be a weakness or dependency on whatever is being abused.....Remember mental over physical.

The great marathon runner, Alberto Salazar once said that a professionally trained distance runner can physically run between eighteen and twenty miles. However, a marathon is twenty-six miles and change. So what happens? According to Salazar, the mind takes charge and wills the body to the finish line. I believe that accomplishing anything, especially change, requires discipline. A major portion of discipline is mental training.

Guideline Number Twenty Nine: Discipline yourself and your child with purpose.

Once upon a time, to discipline someone meant physical punishment for that person. However, we have learned that discipline really addresses one's self-control, obedience, and training. Only after these requirements are met can one be effectively taught anything. This is why many children are not achieving in school. From the outset, they lack discipline and focus. If you were to examine the parents of most under-achieving kids, you would probably find that they lack discipline and focus as well. (The apple and the tree.) Therefore, discipline actually means positioning yourself to take instruction. Once we realize this and begin to direct ourselves in a defined, disciplined manner, we can turn many our dreams into reality.

While attending a mentoring workshop at Franklin High School a few years ago, I was asked to facilitate a group whose topic was academic achievement. During this time, I heard many reasons for students doing well and just as many excuses for them not accomplishing anything of note in school. The statement that stayed with me came from an extremely accomplished young women. Her name was Dr. Anna Law. At the tender age of twenty-six, she had already earned an undergraduate degree, a medical degree and was well on way to graduating with honors for a third degree. She was the top orthodontics student in a class where the next youngest student was in his early thirties! While at

The Teacher In Every Parent

the University of Washington, Dr. Law was also honored as the first African American female ever accepted into the program.

At the workshop, she was asked how she had accomplished so much in such little time. The reason she gave for not yielding to the many pitfalls that befall most young people was simple: She calmly stated two words. DISCIPLINE and FOCUS. She was a very impressive person. Discipline and focus. They can help you change any situation and accomplish anything. I firmly believe that.

When I started working on my dream of becoming a stockbroker, I had no training in that area. I didn't have a sales background. I knew very little about business and even less about stocks, municipal bonds, or mutual funds. I really didn't know how the stock market really worked. Unfortunately for me, there was no role model around to aspire to. The reason I decided to go for that dream was that it sounded good. Little did I realize that most stockbrokers are usually more broke than they are stocked! Nevertheless, I was determined to go for my dream.

I began interviewing in the business district of downtown Seattle and met much resistance. I did not have the right type of experience or background according to most. As I went from firm to firm looking for employment, I knew I had two things going for me. One: I took pride and enthusiasm in hard, smart work. Two: I believed I had ability to sell anything, even with no background-especially myself. I wanted to do something that would give my life value and self-respect. I wanted to have a positive effect on my community. I needed the youngsters in my community to see me and aspire to do the same thing-only better! My goal was to encourage them to realize their dream as well.

I went to several firms and saw where many brokers went to lunch. I merely joined them and politely asked them about their work. I really picked their brains about some of the strategies they utilized to become successful in their field. I then visited the public library and read a great deal of material about becoming a stockbroker. We all know that the library is the least expensive and best source of information available anywhere. I love the library.

Finally, I met the president of a mid-sized brokerage house and convinced him that I could sell an intangible item. Although he was impressed with my enthusiasm and presentation, he said he could not hire me because there were not any current openings. Still determined to achieve my dream, I told the president that I would work for nothing for two weeks! My progress could be monitored daily and if things did not work out, we could just part ways.

At the time, I really could not afford this experiment because I also had a family to support. Fortunately, he agreed and had his assistant give me a reverse directory list to "cold call" from. A cold call, for those who don't know, is an unsolicited, many times unwanted phone call from someone attempting to get you to do something that ordinarily you wouldn't do—mainly, to buy something! The president could afford to do this because he had absolutely nothing to lose. I agreed. The goal of a stockbroker was to call individuals at random and attempt to sell financial investments. I was making one-hundred-fifty phone calls per day with a seventy percent contact ratio and twenty-five percent sales ratio. Two thirds of that group did immediate business with the firm. Two weeks later the assistant to the president came to me with a check for one thousand dollars and offered me a job—as a cold caller! He said I was one of the best phone solicitors he had ever seen.

Not knowing that I had learned something about the business since my brief start, he continued to say that I could 'cold call' for every broker in the office and receive a percentage of everything sold. I politely asked him what his stockbrokers did when they were not selling and was informed that they developed new business. "And how was that done?" I asked. "Predominately by cold calling," was his response. " Well if I'm such a great cold caller, why are you paying me a percentage of what the job is worth and allowing these fat cats to get fatter at my expense? Why don't you just hire yourself another stockbroker?" He chuckled at my suggestion. "You make a good point. Let me think about that one over the weekend." Like I said earlier, my mamma didn't raise no fools.

I got a call on Monday morning. I was hired on Tuesday at three thousand dollars per month to do what I'd been doing for the past three weeks while I studied to take the Series 7 exam in the evening. I was licensed in three months, and although I wasn't the company's odds on to win it, was awarded the firms 'Rookie of the Year' for the year. Next to the Top Company Producer Award, it's an investment firm's top honor. Booked a million-five hundred in business that year. In year two, I accounted for more money than any second-year investment representative the company's history. The fact that I was working during the bull market didn't lessen my achievement in any way, but after a mediocre third year, I decided to resigned. The amount of hours needed to achieve and maintain the status of a top flight stockbroker required too many hours away from my family. (Approximately 80 hours per week.) I had pushed myself too hard. I suddenly needed over the counter stimulants to keep pace with the torrid work agenda I had set. However, my dream was fulfilled and my goal accomplished. The example I set inspired my family as well as the people living in my neighborhood. Later it gave credibility to my tutoring in the community.

A generation ago, Dr. Spock told parents to trust his books when it came to parenting. A line in his now famous child care

Action Plan For Change

manual read: *"You don't know how to parent in the beginning."* Then they introduce us to books that are supposed to do that.

Since the late sixties many "experts" have dispensed volumes of literature advising us as parents. While I don't disagree with his statement entirely, I feel it doesn't give us much credit for having innate parenting skills. I believe it also omits other important steps. Parents must learn to rely on their own ability to trust themselves as caregivers—as well as the books we are reading. That requires time and training. Some have what it takes to parent in the beginning-some don't. During that time however, we should not be negotiating with three years olds!

Dr. Spock obviously had some great ideas and is a true professional in the area of child education. Unfortunately, he thought that parenting could be done using a cookie cutter technique. While some methods of parenting work in general, techniques need to be individualized to fit the child you have. He also didn't consider that 45% of today's parents would be under twenty-one years of age. He also didn't consider that out of the other 55 percent, 35% don't have a extended family to rely on for support. He also probably never considered that 85% of all mothers must work outside the home. Dr. Spock also never considered that passive parenting would backfire in the manner it has. He has gone on record as saying "I may have made a miscalculation," where passive parenting is concerned. He is correct in saying that. He also miscalculated the effect that outside influences would play on the young, fragile, impressionable minds of children. We as parents know a great deal more than anybody else about our children. We don't need to fixate on the so called expertise of professionals whose information usually addresses children in general not yours in particular.

However, today with many young, inexperienced parents, a slightly different strategy should probably be used. I believe the

The Teacher In Every Parent

initial teaching must come from a parent's observation of their kids. Study them and make mental notes. Practice being around your child on a regular basis. After we learn about the ways, attitudes and idiosyncrasies of your own kids, we can utilize many of the good pieces of child-rearing literature that may help enhance the direction of our teaching. We also must prepare ourselves to parent. We must prepare ourselves to lead our children. Many of us have innate parenting skills, but whether we have them or not, they can be taught. Like anything, it takes time, effort and consistency. After which I believe we can be the experts where parenting is concerned. Hence the title of my book. The Teacher in EVERY Parent. As a result, you won't have to rely on any professionals for parenting instruction.

In these times, men have to become more involved in the lives of their children as well. As a man, if you are already doing a great job, you're to be commended but, don't make a big deal out of it. Don't get carried away. As Sonja says, "You're just doing your reasonable service." What we need to know as potential parents, or even as established parents is that the world doesn't always value this difficult task. Today, there isn't much credit given to a good parent—only blame when things go wrong. It's a fact that society doesn't respect parenting as it should; It only pays lip service to it. Legislators pass a bill here, pass a bill there. But our society doesn't really respect children. I'm sorry to say that but I believe it.

Even as society disregards our children, we still need to continue to develop the type of child our communities must have to be successful ones. In spite of the odds we must continue to persevere. Single mothers must continue to be exceptional people. Women have always led and raised families. This notion that woman just started working when they began to draw paychecks is absurd! Parenting successfully is the hardest work of all.

Action Plan For Change

With the need for many women to enter the work place, our children have suffered. A study of working parents suggests that in the last generation alone, the amount of time a parent and children spend together has decreased by 40 percent.

Many jobs in America lack liberal paid family leaves for parents. This makes the notion of 'quality time' seem more important than it really is. Quantity time is the only way children can be raised properly. Until Corporate America wakes up to the importance of the parent and child relationship, it will be up to us parents to produce upstanding, quality children. This world desperately needs more young people of substance and quality to lead it. Let yours and mine be the guide that inspires others to reach the top.

An action plan for change must come from the public and private sectors of business in order to help children to become the upstanding, rational, achieving adults we know they can be.

FROM THOUGHT TO ACTION

As it was explained to me: A thought is a silent word so a word is an exposed thought. Everything in life starts in thought form. It's a thought first.

From a thought an idea is formed. An idea is the second concept of the thought. In other words, the thought has moved into reality.

The third concept is called imagination. Imagination changes the idea into a plan. You may have a hundred ideas a day-everything from what to build, what to wear and what to do. An idea becomes a plan when imagination is added.

The Teacher In Every Parent

The final concept and most important step is the goal. The goal is the written version of an idea. The goal is a documented plan of action. It serves as a constant reminder of what you need to do.

I've been using goals since I was about ten years old. In the beginning, I wrote my ideas down because they seemed to help me concentrate. As I stated earlier I'm an idea person. Ideas basically come from dreaming, which I did sometimes too much as a child. However, I believe dreaming up ideas was the primary impetus for many things I accomplished as a kid.

We should always encouraged bold and ambitious dreaming from our children. We always attempted to set the example of planning and goal setting ourselves in order to achieve our dreams. Jesse Jackson spoke at our high school during the early days of Operation Push. Through everything he said that afternoon, the statement that remained fixed on my mind was, "Whatever one can conceive and believe, one can achieve." Jesse certainly was not the first to make this statement, however, he was the first individual I heard say it and it inspired me to change some dumb things I was doing at the time.

THIRTEEN

THE POWER TO CHANGE

Creating a New and Improved You

If you want your children to be more than they are now, you've got to be more than you are now. Ask yourself what is it that you have to do to get where you want to be? What will you have to know? What new examples will you need to set? You're always going to be reaching for new levels. Remember, however, that you and your young people move hand in hand. You have to improve and they have to witness your improvement; You have to challenge them to improve themselves!

Explain the type of person you desire to become:

Explain the type of person you want your child to become:

What makes you happy? What gives you passion?

What makes your child happy? What gives them passion?

What can you do today to get closer to your child?

CHECKLIST FOR AN IMPROVED LIFE

To become all that you can, you must expand yourself in many areas. Check the places that you have begun to accomplish and add some to this list!

Quit smoking or drinking
Become more physically active
Learn new skills
Make more friends
Become more altruistic
Get more education
Become more spiritual
Get closer to your children
Enjoy more leisure time
Live a meaningful life
Find that dream job
Inspire others
Set solid, well defined goals

Goals are not dreams, they are the beginning of your action plan for success. Write them down and plaster them everywhere. (On your bathroom mirror, on your refrigerator, on the closet door, etc.).
They should be:

Realistic - If you were not born in the United States, it's unrealistic to think that some day you are going to be president of the United States of America. You want them to be attainable goals.

Defined - Clear, concise and accurate goals. "I'm going to sell ten homes this month." If it's not clear, you will not know if you made it or not.

Desirable - Be positive these goals are things you want, because they are going to enrich your life. After all, what we wish for is what creates the passion necessary to achieve it. I call it the fuel in your tank.

For more ideas, see: The Family Creative Workshops, available from Time Life Books.

SUGGESTIONS FOR ADDITIONAL READINGS

* The Cooperating Family, Eleanor- Berman. Prentice-Hall, 1977
* Raising a Responsible Child, Don Dinkmeyer and Gary Mckay. Simon and Schuster, 1973
* Teenagers: The Continuing Challenge, Shirley Gould. Hawthorn Books 1977
* Smarter Kids, Lawrence Greene. I IP Books, Inc. 1987
* Children of Fast Track Parents, Andree' Aelion Brooks 1989
* Prime Time Parenting, Kay Kuzman. R. R. Donnelley & Sons Co., 1980

The Teacher In Every Parent

REFERENCE GUIDE

Superself, Charles Givens; 1994

Family Rules, Kenneth Kaye; 1993

Executive Odessy, Frederick Harmon; 1994

Parents Solution Book, Lea Brammick & Anita Simon; 1993

Understanding Your Potential, Myles Monroe; 1992

What Do You Really Want For Your Children,
Wayne W. Dyer; 1985

We're Driving Our Kids Crazy, Arlie Jean Payne; 1991

Love & Power, Glen Austin; 1988

Quality Parenting, Linda Albert and Mike Popkin; 1987

Getting Along with a New Parent, William L. Coleman; 1992

Smarter Kids, Lawrence J. Greene; 1985

Children of Fast Track Parents, Andree' Aelion Brooks; 1989

Prime Time Parenting, Kay Kuzma, Ed. D.; 1980

How To Raise An Independent Child, Shirley Gould; 1992

Grade School Photos
of the Twins

Top: Joseph Jr. and Jawanna at 17.
Their Great Grandfather O.D. Payne and my Mother, Ruth.
Bottom: The kids at fifteen with cousins Danyelle, Chrisona
and Antonio

1.) Jawanna with Fiancee
2.) Me with buddy,
   Yul Melonson
3.) At A Tennis Event
   With Friends George
   Monroe and Byron
   Washington

4.) Jawanna and Joseph just hanging out

Doing what I love most.
Being close to nature.

My Ace in the whole,
Larry Evans

The Power To Change

About The Author

Joseph P. Smith was born in Fairbanks, Alaska, and currently lives in Atlanta, GA. He is the successful parent of twin young adults who now attend Howard University and the University of Washington. As a businessman, lecturer, and community helper and former teacher, he continues to motivate all people through his leadership and positive examples. You can visit the website at www.Topparent.pyar.com or contact at Jotophiker@.aol.com

SELF HELP NOTES

SELF HELP NOTES

SELF HELP NOTES

SELF HELP NOTES

SELF HELP NOTES

SELF HELP NOTES

SELF HELP NOTES

SELF HELP NOTES

SELF HELP NOTES

SELF HELP NOTES

SELF HELP NOTES

SELF HELP NOTES

SELF HELP NOTES

SELF HELP NOTES

SELF HELP NOTES

SELF HELP NOTES

SELF HELP NOTES

SELF HELP NOTES

SELF HELP NOTES

SELF HELP NOTES